THE GREAT MAN CODE

DISCIPLINE, BROTHERHOOD, AND THE RETURN TO STILLNESS

For the daughter who will inherit the world disciplined men rebuild.

For Layla.

You arrived, and my standards rose.
Not from pressure — from clarity.

May you always be protected by men who govern themselves,
and never have to search the world to recognize steady love.

If you ever wonder what kind of man your father chose to be,
live beside me. You will see it.

You are not why I became strong.
You are why I refused to remain anything less.

—Dad

AUTHOR'S NOTE— TO THE MEN WHO STILL STAND

This book was written for the man who refuses to collapse.

Who learned, often alone, that the world does not reward quiet strength. It requires it.

If that is you, understand this now:

Suffering does not make a man rare. Staying on his feet does.

I wrote *The Great Man Code* because I lived too many years without a structure strong enough to hold me when emotion surged and chaos demanded reaction.

I have been the boy holding tension together while everything around him fractured.

The man betrayed and forced into clarity.

The leader who discovered that discipline is not restriction. It is protection.

A scar, a lesson, a law.

Those laws became this Code. Structure.

Because when a man has no structure, he negotiates with weakness. When he lives by law, he becomes harder to move.

We live in a time that mistakes outrage for courage and distraction for freedom.

Real strength has order to it. It does not spill everywhere.

A disciplined man does not suppress emotion. He sequences it. He feels fully, then acts from clarity.

The Great Man Code is divided into four domains. The Code, The House, The Brotherhood, and The Kingdom.

This is not intensity for its own sake. It is direction.

The aim is precision.

When a man governs himself, very little in this world can govern him.

If you came here for comfort, you will not find it.

If you came here for clarity, you will.

Somewhere in these pages, you recognize the man you were before the noise.

The one still standing, but not yet ordered.

A man who governs himself becomes a structure the world can lean on.

The world does not repair itself.

But disciplined men rebuild it, first within, then everywhere they stand.

CONTENTS

Introduction—The Structure Of A Great Man 9

THE CODE

Chapter 1. The Death Of The Modern Man.. 21

Chapter 2. The Forge 31

Chapter 3. The Law Of Order. 41

Chapter 4. The Oath Of Restraint... 51

Chapter 5. The Foundation Of Presence 61

Chapter 6. The Code. 69

THE HOUSE

Chapter 7. The Law Of The Arena. 79

Chapter 8. The Man In Stillness... 89

Chapter 9. The Oath Of The House... 97

Chapter 10. The Law Of Polarity. 107

Chapter 11. The Oath Of Endurance.. 121

Chapter 12. The Oath Of Purpose.. 139

Chapter 13. The Oath Of Kingship 155

THE BROTHERHOOD

Chapter 14. The Oath Of Brotherhood.. 171

Chapter 15. The Brotherhood 181

THE KINGDOM

Chapter 16. The Oath Of The Kingdom 203

Chapter 17. The Law Of Eternity 217

The Mirror **241**

INTRODUCTION—
THE STRUCTURE OF
A GREAT MAN

A man without structure eventually breaks under his own weight.

The Great Man Code is a blueprint for building a life that stands when everything else collapses.

Each domain tests a different part of you.

Each one introduces laws to live by, reflections to wrestle with, and anchors, short true stories that prove The laws in practice.

Together, they form a cycle.

Master yourself.

Order your home.

Strengthen your Brotherhood.

Then carry it into the world without ego.

The Structure

Book I: The Code The Foundation

You will build discipline, purpose, and emotional control.

You will learn that a man's first law is mastery over his own reaction.

Book II: The House The Order

> You will build order in your home, relationships, and peace. Leadership meets protection here.

Book III: The Brotherhood The Circle

> Brotherhood becomes accountability, loyalty, and correction.

Book IV: The Kingdom The Legacy

> You build systems that outlast you and find peace independent of control.

Each book ends with an oath, a promise between you and the discipline that made you.

Everything you read has a purpose, to forge you into a man of clarity, composure, and calm strength.

Greatness is quiet, repeatable, and structured.

Lead yourself first, and everything you touch will carry the weight of your steadiness.

A man who governs himself can bring order wherever he stands.

This Code was not written to make men better than others.

It was written to make them whole again.

How to Read This Book

Do not rush it.

Read one section, then apply it before moving on. This book is meant to be lived, not finished.

Carry a pen. Underline what hits.

When a passage stings, stop. That one is for you.

The Code is structure.

Adapt it. Refine it. Live it.

Then return when life exposes where you only understood it on paper.

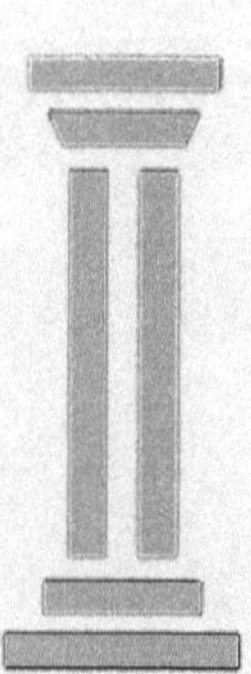

BOOK I

THE CODE

BEFORE YOU CAN LEAD ANYONE,
YOU MUST MASTER YOURSELF.
DISCIPLINE IS THE FORGE WHERE
WEAKNESS BURNS.

The Quiet Collapse

Your armor will crack. Not in battle. In silence.

You wake with no hunger, no purpose, no edge. You tell people you are fine. Work is fine. The relationship is fine.

But fine is a tomb with good lighting. Men die in it all the time.

Falling apart can feel peaceful. That is what makes it dangerous. Only a steady leak until the heat is gone.

The warrior becomes the spectator. The leader becomes the pleaser.

I know that silence. It does not roar. It hums.

You start thinking calm is the goal.

Stand up.

The fall is only fatal if you stay there.

The Disease of Ease

Ease gave us everything except the resistance required to feel alive. Numb ambition is the first symptom. Hunger erodes. Action slows. Excuses speed up.

Moral drift follows. Lines you once refused to cross start moving. Discipline loosens. Standards negotiate. What once felt unthinkable becomes manageable.

Then comes distraction disguised as connection. Digital dopamine replaces earned significance. You scroll, you consume, you react. But you do not advance.

Ease replaces purpose with options and calls it freedom. But freedom without restraint is not liberation. It is drift. You cannot aim for a life built entirely around avoiding discomfort.

We have more tools, more opportunity, more knowledge than any generation before us. And yet we produce weaker men. Because we have removed the friction that forges them.

A man should rest after he bleeds, not instead of it.

Without contrast, gratitude dies, and when gratitude dies, meaning follows.

When you train your body, deny your comfort, keep your word, sit in silence, you are performing the same ritual men have done for thousands of years. You are proving to yourself that comfort serves you. It does not own you.

That is the antidote to the disease: earned peace. Peace that comes after resistance, not instead of it.

The moment you choose discomfort on purpose, you break the hold of ease.

Strength has always offended the weak. But you know better now.

You have seen what comfort does to the untested. It takes the fire out of their eyes and replaces it with flickering screens. It trades their roar for a polite nod. It teaches them to fear their own capability.

Would you still be proud of who you are if the world stripped away every comfort tomorrow?

If the answer makes you hesitate, you already know where we are heading next.

The Weight of Silence

You are carrying a silence the world will never hear.

I learned this early.

When my brother died, I made a silent pact with myself: do not break.

I remember answering people in a flat voice because if anything cracked, I did not trust it would stop.

No tears. No weakness. No visible fracture.

It looked like strength.

Every quiet night felt like judgment.

I turned pain into posture and called it resilience.

It was not resilience. It was repression.

Silence is only strength when it is chosen.

But unspoken pain does not disappear. It compounds. You can hide from emotion, but it will not hide from you.

It shows up in your temper. In your exhaustion. In the distance between you and the people who love you.

The same stillness that suffocates the untrained man strengthens the disciplined one. When chosen deliberately, silence becomes a weapon. It removes noise, distraction, and fear until all that remains is the voice you buried beneath it.

When you sit in silence by choice, you are not suppressing emotion. You are confronting it. You are saying, "Speak. Show me what is still wounded."

That is not weakness. That is mastery.

The quiet collapse is the modern man's initiation. A man must learn to hear his own thoughts before he earns the right to act on them.

The weight of silence, then, is both a burden and a teacher. It will test your patience, expose your fear, and reveal the parts of you still built on noise. If you can learn to stand still in it, to let it scrape you clean without reaching for a distraction, something beneath it becomes clear: a quieter, steadier voice.

So do not rush to fill it. Do not reach for the noise to drown it out. Sit in it until you can tell the difference between the silence that kills you and the silence that makes you ready.

The first sound that breaks true silence is not a scream or a cry. It is a vow.

And it starts here.

The Collapse Without Witness

Men no longer collapse in public. They disappear.

They fade quietly, behind polite smiles. The world no longer witnesses a man's breaking. It scrolls past it.

A man can look functional while dying inside. He can hold a job. Pay bills. Post family photos, and still feel invisible.

We live in an era where men are not allowed to bleed. Pain is pathologized. Strength is misinterpreted. Weakness is rebranded as virtue. We have built a culture that confuses vulnerability with exposure. A man's real breakdown, the raw kind that precedes transformation, makes people uncomfortable. So instead of help, he gets labels.

And so the modern man learns to suffer quietly. He performs competence while his mind drifts to the question that keeps him awake at night: What happened to me?

Somewhere along the way, you stopped recognizing yourself.

The truth is simple. No one saw you fall because no one was watching.

Everyone is busy performing their own image of stability. The world does not slow down for a man who loses his footing. It steps over him. It is a reminder that no one is coming to save you.

No one witnesses your collapse but you. It buys your next evolution. The world is not supposed to understand it. It is supposed to see who walks back out afterward.

If you feel unseen, good. Solitude is where the mask melts. Isolation is where identity reforges. Every man who has ever led anything worth following was first ignored, doubted, or mocked. That invisibility is the crucible. Proof that your worth is not determined by witness, but by will.

You are being hidden for construction. You are being rebuilt without witnesses so you will never again need them.

So let the world ignore you. Let the noise move on without you. Stay in the shadows long enough for your foundations to harden.

Because when you return, you will not be looking for validation. You will be looking for purpose.

The Code does not start when the world finally notices you again.

It starts now, in the dark, while you rebuild unseen.

When collapse happens without witnesses, a man faces what older cultures once called initiation.

No audience means no performance left to hide behind.

The Missing Rite

Every culture that has ever raised strong men has given them a trial. The Spartans had the agōgē, where boys were stripped of comfort and forged through hunger, cold, and consequence until only discipline remained. The Lakota sent their sons into solitude to fast and pray until fear either broke them or clarified them. Samurai carved their code into steel and repetition, knowing that hesitation meant death. Even the village blacksmith's apprentice understood the burn of apprenticeship, that mastery was earned through heat, repetition, and sacrifice long before recognition. These were not traditions. They were filters. And we removed them.

Initiation never disappears. It only changes terrain. We told boys they could become men through age, paperwork, or a paycheck. We replaced trial with comfort and called it progress. But when a society stops testing its men, life does it instead. Quietly. Without warning. Through collapse, pressure, and silence that does not explain itself. You've already felt it. That moment where nothing held, where no one stepped in, where something in you either hardened or avoided the weight. That was it.

The old tribes understood something modern men try to escape: a man who has not faced himself under pressure is dangerous, not only to others, but to everything he claims to protect. So they built the trial to remove immaturity, arrogance, and dependence before responsibility was ever given. Today, that removal happens without guidance. The collapse you've lived through was not random. It was initiation without structure.

Every culture demanded confrontation, whether through wilderness, weapon, or weakness. When a man faces what can break him and stands anyway, he stops waiting for permission to live. That is why no one applauds it. That is why no one explains it. The absence of a witness is what makes it real. The man who endures without recognition is the man who no longer needs it. He stops performing and starts embodying. And that is where men separate. Not at success. At structure.

Pain was never the enemy. It was always the language. It does not only wound. It clarifies. It burns away what cannot hold weight and leaves only what can. The world will tell you to numb it. The Code demands you use it. Because pain is the proof that something in you is still capable of change.

The rites did not disappear. They adapted.

The missing rite is not missing anymore.

You're standing in it.

From this point forward, you either pass through it deliberately—

or you repeat it unconsciously.

The Code Awakens

Your life does not change when you learn something new. It changes when you stop negotiating with what you already know. Before that moment, you move by reaction, pulled by impulse, comfort, and opinion. After it, you move by law, not rules imposed on you, but standards you enforce whether anyone sees them or not.

This is not a philosophy. It is recognition.

Men once learned these laws through pressure, mentorship, and consequence. They were not written. They were lived. Discipline was expected. Order was required. Authority was earned. Legacy was built. Time was respected. When those structures disappeared, men did not become free. They became unanchored.

You've seen it. In others. In yourself.

That's where The Code begins.

Not when you agree with it.

When you stop avoiding it.

The initiation is not ahead of you. It already happened. You faced collapse. You endured silence. You saw what comfort does when it goes unchecked. You are not starting from nothing. You are starting from exposure.

Architecture requires law. That is what The Code restores. Not motivation. Not intensity. Structure. Something that holds when emotion does not.

The laws are simple:

Discipline: you command yourself under pressure.

Order: you build structure that holds without you.

Authority: you lead through restraint and example.

Legacy: you build strength that survives you.

Mortality: you act knowing time does not wait.

You don't learn these once. You live them repeatedly. At higher levels. Under greater pressure. The man who thinks he is finished is already declining.

This is not about perfection. It never was.

It is about alignment.

The Code does not make you louder. It makes you precise. It does not make you visible. It makes you undeniable.

The old ways were never lost.

They were abandoned.

And now they are waiting for men willing to carry them again.

No one is coming to initiate you.

No system will enforce this.

No audience will reward it.

That is the point.

Because the moment a man accepts that responsibility, everything changes.

He stops searching.

He starts enforcing.

And from that point forward, the measure of his life is no longer how he feels—

but how he stands.

CHAPTER 1

THE DEATH OF THE MODERN MAN

Section 1: The Autopsy

Every age buries its men differently. Ours buries them politely.

No war. No famine. No plague. Only the slow suffocation of comfort.

The modern man did not die on a battlefield. He died on a couch. He was conquered by convenience. Shoulders built for weight. Eyes meant to scan horizons. The structure remains, but the tension is gone. The spine softened under negotiation with ease.

First, ambition was replaced with entertainment. Duty became optional. Faith became ironic. Silence filled with noise. He was told strength was aggression and leadership oppression, so he apologized for his instincts. He turned the blade inward, filing down every sharp edge until nothing remained that could protect.

The tragedy is not that modern men are bad. It is that they are untested.

Their muscles have never trembled under real weight. And without resistance, potential rots. The autopsy reveals neglect, not malice. The body of modern man shows no mortal wound, only atrophy.

He wasn't murdered. He decayed.

And if you're honest, you've felt it happening in real time. Not collapse. Slow permission.

Look at the corpse. The hands are clean because they've built nothing. The eyes are dull from watching everything. The heart is faint because it's been numbed by constant stimulation.

This is abundance without discipline. The paradox of progress. Civilization promised him liberation. It delivered sedation. He has food. Shelter. Endless entertainment, yet he wakes with dread.

Comfort cannot replace mission. A man needs something to fight for. Without that, his power turns inward and corrodes him.

We examine what failed, not to wallow in decay but to learn what must be rebuilt. Cause of death: loss of resistance.

He stopped pushing back against distraction, against conformity, against the parts of himself that begged for indulgence. Every time he chose comfort over challenge, he weakened the instinct that once defined him.

What a man refuses to test, he eventually loses.

He avoids it once. Then again. Then it becomes who he is.

Somewhere deep down, the instinct remains, the need to test himself, provide, protect, lead. Buried under years of sedation, but not dead. You feel it in sudden moments: a reflection that startles you, a crisis that clarifies you. Decisive. Calm. Alive. That is the man waiting to return. Or the man you already buried.

Before resurrection comes rot. That's what The Code demands: truth before transformation. Until you admit the body is cold, you cannot summon life back into it.

So take one last look at the dead man, the version of yourself who lived by avoidance, excuse, and sedation. See him clearly. Then close his eyes. From this point forward, we stop embalming the corpse. We rebuild the man.

Section 2: The Symptoms

He can hold a conversation while checking his phone, nod through a family dinner while scrolling through the lives of strangers.

Comfort addiction is the first symptom. Comfort has a logic of its own: it whispers that every hard thing can wait. An extra hour of sleep. An extra scroll before bed. A skipped workout justified as "rest."

Each decision feels harmless until the small comforts form an ecosystem. The bed becomes the throne, the screen becomes the altar. Tomorrow never comes. And eventually, neither does the man you thought you'd become.

Avoid discomfort long enough, and you become unfit for it. And once he's allergic to discomfort, he's unfit for greatness. Not temporarily. Permanently, if nothing changes.

The second symptom is confusion. He's told to "be himself," but no one tells him what that means. He's told to lead, but also to obey; to be vulnerable, but never weak; to protect, but never offend. Contradiction paralyzes him. A confused man seeks permission. Unable to anchor himself in anything permanent, he floats. Chasing validation from the very world that broke him.

Confusion turns strength into performance. The modern man lifts weights, but not burdens. He learns quotes, but not conviction. He talks about mental toughness while outsourcing every hard choice to convenience. He wears the uniform of discipline but not its scars. He doesn't know who he serves anymore.

The third symptom is comparison. He compares salaries. Physiques. Followers. Lifestyles. Metrics designed to inflame insecurity. Every scroll becomes a reminder that someone else is stronger, richer, freer. It does not inspire. It corrodes.

Comparison shifts a man from mission to measurement. Comparison is the great thief of masculine peace. And when judgment turns inward, it becomes shame, the quiet poison that makes a man hide from the very actions that would redeem him.

Together they form the modern trinity of weakness: comfort, confusion, comparison. Comfort dulls the senses, confusion blurs direction, and comparison kills gratitude. This is not oppression. It is erosion.

The result is a generation of physically capable, intellectually overstimulated, spiritually empty men. He knows more but is less. He achieves more but feels less. He lives longer but matters less.

That is the insult of the age: capacity everywhere, command nowhere. You can feel that in your own life.

Every man hits a wall, an emotional collision where comfort, confusion, and comparison all fail him at once. He looks around and realizes he's surrounded by noise yet completely alone. That's when the choice appears: continue dying slowly, or start rebuilding deliberately.

If the first section was an autopsy, this one is a diagnosis. The body can still live. But only if we stop lying about what is killing it.

Section 3: The Root Cause

It came from decades of conditioning. He wasn't corrupted by vice; he was domesticated by comfort. Remove struggle, and strength disappears. Remove purpose, and endurance goes with it. Remove discipline, and consequence means nothing.

What remains is not a villain. It is a man who has forgotten why he exists. When survival became easy, meaning became optional. So they grew up aware, but weak. Aware enough to see it. Too weak to correct it.

The final blow was the erosion of fathers and mentors. When men disappeared from homes, the transmission of wisdom broke. No one told them that restraint and empathy can coexist, that power and gentleness aren't enemies.

Modern men drift because they are trying to live a masculine life in a culture that calls masculinity a disease. He can't win by being strong and can't respect himself by being weak.

So he becomes acceptable. Then he wonders why he feels absent. Because he is.

The world did not steal masculinity. Men surrendered it. The Code begins not with blame, but ownership. No one is coming to fix it.

Responsibility reconnects him to consequence. Freedom is not the absence of burden. It is the mastery of it.

You don't need the world to return to old values; you need to embody them yourself. The root cause is disconnection. The cure is responsibility: reconnection to effort, brotherhood, faith, and consequence. When a man reclaims them, he stops being a byproduct of his culture and becomes its correction.

Section 4: The Moment of Truth

The moment of truth comes when a man stops running from his own reflection. It happens in silence. On an ordinary morning when the noise runs out. You sit at the edge of the bed and feel the weight of honesty pressing into your chest. No one has to tell you what is wrong. You already know.

Recognition cuts. It is the moment you realize the enemy is not the world. It is your surrender to it. You built an identity around survival, not strength. The worst part is not that you fell. It is that you stopped fighting to rise.

Every man faces this mirror. But the pattern is the same: the world holds up a reflection of the man you became, and you realize he's not the one you were meant to be. Then the voice inside you speaks. It does not argue. It does not explain. It says one word: "Enough." Now.

That word is mercy only if you obey it. Ignore it, and it becomes a sentence.

When a man owns what he has become, he stops being ruled by it. This is the burial. The Code doesn't begin with a new identity. It begins with a funeral. Bury the man who obeys weakness before you build the man who commands strength. Decide now whether the man you are will be buried or rebuilt. Most men do not act here. They adjust. And that adjustment is where they disappear.

THE MAN WHO REFUSED

He saw the mirror and turned on a softer light. Told himself he was tired. That everyone slows down eventually. That pressure changes a man. He stopped waking before the alarm. Stopped loading the bar the way he used to. Left the harder conversation for tomorrow. He told himself it was temporary.

His wife noticed first. Not all at once. In little ways. The kind you miss while you're still calling it stress. Not with accusation. With adjustment. She stopped leaning into him when something felt heavy. Stopped asking what he thought before making decisions. Stopped waiting for him to choose.

At work he was dependable. He answered emails. He met deadlines. He was never the man the room shifted toward. Never the one people waited on.

His children adapted quickly. They brought their questions to their mother. Their risks to their friends. They learned his moods before they learned his standards.

He blamed the hours. The culture. The weight of responsibility. He never blamed the compromise. His body thickened at the waist. The weight he once carried in his shoulders settled lower. He still talked about discipline. Still admired strong men online. Still said, "I used to be different." And everyone around him silently agreed.

One evening he sat in a quiet house that still carried his name on the mailbox. The television hummed. No one asked him what to do next. No one waited for him to decide. No one leaned against him when the day felt heavy.

There was no betrayal. No scandal.

Just a man who had lowered his standards often enough that no one felt their loss.

He did not collapse.

He was no longer needed.

How straight you stand with nothing under you decides everything.

No title. No audience. No applause.

Eventually, he stops being shaken.

Or he learns to live permanently unstable.

Reflection

Am I rebuilding or embalming?
There is no third option.

LAW I — DISCIPLINE

Discipline

You command yourself under pressure.

Pressure reveals the man who can command himself.

Or it exposes that you cannot.

CHAPTER 2

THE FORGE

Section 1: The Anvil and the Flame

Every man who decides to rebuild must pass through fire. You've avoided it before.

The Forge is the process of voluntary hardship used to reshape a man's character. The same pressure that removes weakness gives you shape. Iron does not choose the flame. The craftsman does. You are both the iron and the smith now.

Every man needs an anvil: something unmovable to strike himself against. For some it is faith. For others, family, purpose, or principle. Without an anvil, blows scatter. With one, they shape.

Discipline is the strike. Repetition is the shaping. You don't negotiate with it. You submit to it until form appears.

Every man remembers his first forge. The first time he stayed in the heat when quitting would have been easier. The first time he learned that escape always charges interest. The old self breaks before anything stronger can form.

Build your forge deliberately. Choose your anvil. Choose your flame. Enter daily.

The Forge does not care whether you are inspired. It cares whether you return.

The Forge is sacred because it is earned. It is the gym at dawn, the quiet prayer before chaos, the last rep when no one is watching, the call you do not want to make. You do not rise from fire polished. You rise unfinished, stronger, truer.

Enter The Forge. Or stay the same.

Order is what allows strength to endure.

ORIGIN OF DISCIPLINE

He was fifteen when silence first became armor.

There was only the sound of adults breaking behind closed doors. His little brother was gone, declared dead before the night could make sense of itself. People arrived with lowered voices and careful hands, asking what they could do. No embrace could reverse time. No word could occupy the space where a laugh used to live.

He looked at his mother, hollowed. He looked at his father, undone.

In that moment he understood something without being taught:

they were already breaking.

So he buried it.

He did not cry, not because the pain was absent, but because someone had to remain standing.

I remember answering people in a flat voice, because if anything cracked, I did not trust it would stop.

Do not add to the noise when others are drowning.

That night he decided emotion would not master him.

And every day after, he paid for it again.

In the weeks that followed, the house fell quiet. He answered softly, moved deliberately, made himself smaller so nothing else would fracture. Friends spoke. Teachers asked questions he refused to entertain.

What he wanted was not comfort.

It was control.

He could not change what happened, but he could decide how far its echo would travel.

Without realizing it, he began constructing the stillness that would later define him: composure inside chaos, restraint under pressure, discipline when emotion demanded release.

Sometimes the bravest thing a man can do is remain upright while everything inside him is falling.

He held himself together because someone had to remain unbroken.

And in that stillness, the boy encountered the man he would spend the rest of his life becoming.

Some men are taught discipline.

Others are forced into it.

You don't get to choose forever.

Section 2: The Death of Motivation

Motivation lies. You've waited for it anyway.

It tells you progress depends on feeling ready. If your performance depends on mood, you will never master anything. It does not survive pressure. Men mistake the spark for the flame.

Discipline begins where motivation ends. It does not ask how you feel. It asks whether you will keep your word. It grows under resistance, especially when no one is impressed by your effort.

Motivation is borrowed energy. Discipline is owned energy. A man of The Code does not chase hype. He cultivates order.

Action produces proof. Proof reshapes identity. Identity demands repetition. Belief does not precede movement. Movement creates belief.

Stop bargaining. Execute.

Emotion serves mission. It does not lead it. Discipline doesn't make life easier. It enables you to handle a harder life without complaint.

Discipline is quiet aggression. Motion without permission. When motivation dies, excuses should die with it.

If they don't, you never were.

Section 3: The Law of Resistance

Every man wants to grow until resistance shows up. That's where most of them stop.

It is not punishment. It is proof you are alive. Everything strong is forged through friction.

A muscle atrophies without tension. Resistance appears before expansion.

Fatigue. Temptation. Doubt. Distraction.

Resistance is not a no. It is a question: "Do you want this badly enough?" Your answer is in what you do next.

The path of least resistance leads to mediocrity.

Resistance appears in three forms:

Physical: strain the body beyond ease. Lift heavier. Run farther. Breathe harder.

Mental: discipline attention. Read before scrolling. Plan before reacting.

Spiritual: hold silence. Sit long enough to hear your own conscience.

Modern society treats pain as a malfunction. But pain has always been a form of language. It reveals where attention is required. The man of The Code does not run from pain. He translates it.

Pain is not the enemy. It is the compass.

The untrained man curses the weight. The disciplined man thanks it.

Seek controlled resistance daily: cold showers, hard conversations, disciplined routines, voluntary discomfort. You are not punishing yourself. You are preparing yourself.

Or it's already gone.

Section 4: Building Ritual

A disciplined man does not rise by chance. He rises by rhythm. You already know what yours looks like.

The warrior prayed before battle. The craftsman sharpened his tools before dawn. The monk rose in darkness. These were not habits. They were rehearsals.

A man with ritual does not negotiate with laziness.

The Sacred Minimum

Most men fail because they aim for perfection instead of permanence. Your sacred minimum is the smallest repeatable unit of excellence you perform every single day, no matter what.

30 minutes of physical exertion. 10 minutes of reflection or prayer. 1 act of integrity.

That is enough. If you actually do it.

Every man has two gates: morning and night. Guard them both. If your discipline depends on ideal conditions, it is not real.

A man with ritual cannot be easily manipulated. If your structure collapses under stress, it wasn't a structure. It was a preference.

The Ritual Test

What do you do when no one is watching? What pattern governs your mornings and nights? Do bad days erase your system?

Ritual is how the man of The Code worships. Because greatness isn't found in bursts of effort. It's carved in repetition.

Or it never gets built at all.

Section 5: Tempered in Fire

Every man carries weight.

Most men try to put it down.

Discipline is what makes that possible. It doesn't erase hardship. It converts it.

Some men melt in heat. Others become steel. The burden becomes proof. The weight isn't the problem. The man who refuses to carry it is.

The disciplined man does not ask for relief. He asks for responsibility.

Some days it feels heavy.

Carry it anyway.

Because no one else will.

He no longer waits for circumstances to get easier, because he has become harder to break. You stop asking, "Why me?" You start saying, "Try me."

The burden does not change. You do.

Carry what's yours. Or prove you never could.

Reflection

If motivation never returns, will I still act?

LAW II — ORDER

Order

You build structure (mission, systems, standards).

Without structure, you drift. Every time.

No structure. No progress.

CHAPTER 3
THE LAW OF ORDER

Section 1: Foundations Before Walls

Every structure stands only as long as its foundation holds.

Men forget this more than most. They start stacking walls. Money, titles, possessions, status. All of it built on soil that's still soft. Then one storm comes, and everything they built tilts.

The world celebrates walls. The Code celebrates foundations. No one applauds a foundation. It still determines everything above it.

If you build on soft ground, you don't get a warning. You get a collapse.

The foundation has three layers: clarity, values, and self-respect.

Clarity: Knowing What You're Building For

Most men build lives they never consciously chose. They chase growth but cannot define direction. Without clarity, every victory feels empty because it was never aimed.

Clarity does not come from a vision board. It comes from confrontation.

Sit in silence long enough to ask yourself uncomfortable questions. What kind of man am I becoming? What am I willing to sacrifice for meaning? What would I still do if no one applauded?

If you do not define the why, every how will betray you.

Values: The Rebar Beneath the Concrete

Values are the reinforcement beneath the structure.

Define three or four non-negotiables. Principles you will bleed for, not just talk about. Honesty. Discipline. Loyalty. Faith.

Let them govern.

You can fail publicly and still stand tall if you never betray your core. Betray your values once, and even success will taste like rust.

Self-Respect: The Weight That Hardens the Mix

Every promise you keep to yourself pours another layer.

Men who skip this step build on approval instead of integrity. Self-respect is the knowledge that you earned your peace.

The Slow Work

Building a foundation is not exciting. It is sacred.

It is the phase no one sees. The repetition. The early mornings. The failures corrected in silence.

Boredom tests devotion.

Anyone can begin when witnessed. Few finish unwatched.

That is why the world has more dreamers than builders. Dreamers love vision. Builders love structure.

Depth first. Height later.

The Blueprint

For men, that blueprint is a mission.

A man who rushes to build walls will spend his life repairing cracks. The man who ignores it rebuilds his life forever.

Section 2: The Mission Blueprint

A man without a mission is a loaded weapon without a target. Drift.

Discipline without direction turns into obsession. Direction without discipline turns into fantasy.

The union of the two is mission.

Why Mission Matters

Goals end. Mission does not.

You finish the project. Buy the car. Hit the milestone. Still wake up restless.

Mission does not end with completion. It survives it.

If your mission cannot survive a hard day, it was never yours. It was convenience dressed as purpose.

Mission Triangle: Purpose, Direction, Discipline

Purpose answers why you exist. What problem do you exist to solve?

Direction answers where you are heading. What does your purpose look like in motion?

Discipline answers how you move. What are you willing to do daily to prove it?

Direction without discipline is drift.

Discipline without purpose is slavery.

The Question That Builds Clarity

I have had mornings where one honest sentence on paper did more than a week of thinking.

If I died in ten years, what work would I regret not completing?

Who benefits if I win?

Mission is who your excellence serves.

The man who fights only for himself runs out of reason. The man who fights for something larger runs out of excuses.

From Goals to Systems of Aim

A goal says you will make a million. A mission says you will master value creation.

A goal says you will get fit. A mission says you become the man who keeps promises to his body.

Connect every objective back to the blueprint.

Does this serve my purpose?

Does this align with my direction?

Does this require discipline?

If not, leave it.

The Written Blueprint

The Code demands your mission in writing.

A spoken dream disappears. A written one shapes action.

Keep it short enough to remember and heavy enough to matter.

If it does not move your blood, it is not truth. It is marketing.

Once written, let it decide your schedule, your circle, your sacrifices.

Common Pitfalls of the Builder

Building without a blueprint.

Acting first, clarifying later.

Building for applause.

Validation creates weak mortar.

Building without measurement.

What is not tracked decays.

Building alone.

The Oath of Mission

"I will not mistake movement for meaning. If I build fast and hollow, I accept the collapse that follows."

Without it, you're just moving in place.

Section 3: Systems Over Feelings

A mission without systems is a wish.

A man without systems is a slave to emotion. You've lived that cycle.

I learned that the hard way. The days I had no structure were the days I drifted fastest.

Every choice leaks energy.

When your life runs on systems, you do not try to stay aligned. You are built that way.

You do not hope to work out. You train at a set time.

You do not try to focus. Your phone leaves the room.

You do not plan to save money. It happens automatically.

He does not argue with emotion. He removes emotion from the equation.

Most men do not fail because they lack discipline. They fail because they never designed their lives to require it. So when pressure comes, they fold.

Hierarchy

Ritual becomes routine. Routine becomes system. System becomes legacy.

The builder turns grit into architecture.

He does not just act with discipline. He designs it.

Designing Systems for the Four Pillars

Body: movement, fuel, rest. Schedule workouts like meetings. Keep a fixed wake time. Treat your body as the workshop.

Mind: input, focus, reflection. Control your information diet. Read what reinforces strength. End each day with reflection.

Spirit: stillness, gratitude, conviction. Create space for silence. Align actions with values. Serve something larger.

Mission: structure, accountability, review. Break mission into measurable projects. Track weekly. Review quarterly.

Emotion as Interference

Feelings are data. Not commands.

Fatigue says rest with purpose, not quit.

Fear says proceed with precision, not retreat.

Anger says correct the problem, not explode.

The Code does not ask how you feel. It asks if you did it.

From System to Freedom

Structure creates freedom.

A man with systems does not live in a cage. He lives without chaos.

Every system you build is a promise to your future self.

Or you will keep breaking where structure should have held you.

Section 4: Order Beyond the Self

Chaos begins on the edges. A messy workspace. A skipped task. A relationship without boundaries.

Then it takes you with it.

The man of The Code keeps his perimeter clean.

What you tolerate becomes what surrounds you. You chose more of it than you admit.

Order in the Environment

Your surroundings reflect your mind.

Disorder is not random. It is residue.

Folding clothes. Wiping counters. Organizing tools. These are not chores.

They are declarations.

I have had nights where resetting one room kept my head from going sideways.

Order that cannot survive inside a home is not order at all.

Order in Relationships

Most men do not fail from enemies. They fail from tolerated company.

Keep the men who sharpen you. Remove the ones who dull you.

A strong Brotherhood refines. It does not flatter.

You do not need many. You need alignment.

Order in Boundaries

A disciplined man protects energy.

Every yes that violates your mission is a betrayal. And you feel it every time.

Once you stop needing approval, you become free to serve what matters.

Order as Spiritual Alignment

Order without humility becomes tyranny.

Strength serves. It does not dominate.

Or it collapses the moment you do.

Section 5: Peace Is Architecture

Peace is not discovered.

It is constructed.

Peace is not the absence of pressure. It is control under pressure.

Peace begins when standards become immovable.

You cannot tolerate contradiction and claim tranquility.

The man of The Code does not ask the world to quiet down. He builds himself until storms sound familiar.

If your structure is weak, peace will always be temporary.

The Peace Oath

"I do not seek peace from the world. I build it within myself, then expand it outward. If peace leaves, I audit my structure, not the storm."

Reflection

Where in my life have I mistaken chaos for freedom?

LAW III — AUTHORITY

Authority

You lead by example and restraint.

Authority is earned through the restraint others can feel.

If you cannot restrain yourself, you cannot lead.

CHAPTER 4

THE OATH OF RESTRAINT

Section 1: The Weight of Command

What a man builds eventually demands to be led. You've already felt that pressure.

Every man dreams of leadership until he carries it. Your reactions become instruction. Your discipline becomes culture.

Leadership is not granted by title. It is verified under strain. When pressure rises, men watch what you do more than what you say.

I've watched a room tighten because one man lost his tone for three seconds. The leader's calm is contagious. So is his chaos.

The Mirror Principle

Every leader eventually meets himself through the reflection of his team, family, and tribe. Their discipline mirrors his own. Their confusion mirrors his drift. Their courage mirrors his conviction.

The first task of leadership is self-governance.

If you panic, they scatter. If you lash out, they hide. If you stay measured, even in failure, they learn steadiness from your silence.

A man teaches most when he is being tested.

The man of The Code never expects loyalty he has not earned.

The Burden of Visibility

The higher you rise, the less freedom you have to act on impulse. One careless word from a leader carries more weight than a thousand from the crowd. You cannot afford to vent like the men you guide.

Your emotions are not private anymore. They are precedent.

Every man who commands must decide: Do I want to feel understood or be effective?

Command as Stewardship

Leadership is not control. It is custody. That is why arrogance destroys more leaders than weakness ever could. When pride enters command, stewardship turns into domination.

The Emotional Economy of Command

Every reaction either fuels or drains the system. The leader must give strength without hemorrhaging it. Stillness is strategy. Reflection is recovery. You are the one who sets the rhythm.

Rest is not indulgence. It is maintenance of precision.

Leading by Presence

A man's presence leads louder than his words. When he walks in with quiet certainty, men straighten. When he listens more than he speaks, they measure their own noise.

You do not demand respect. You draw it.

Or it exposes that he never had it.

Section 2: Influence

Leadership is not measured by how loudly you speak, but by what happens when you stop speaking. You've seen what follows you.

The Triad of Influence: Example → Respect → Authority

Most men try to reverse this order. They demand before they have disciplined. The void is the invoice for boundaries you never enforced.

Respect earned through example becomes unshakeable authority. Without it, nothing you say holds.

Example shows up in stupid little moments: how you answer when you are tired, how you handle being interrupted, whether your tone changes when you do not get your way.

A man's influence is the echo of his habits.

Emotional Control: The Signal of Strength

The strongest man in the room is not the one who speaks first. It is the one whose pulse stays steady when everyone else panics.

People follow calm because calm feels like competence.

The Code calls this the temperature rule: The leader sets the emotional temperature of the tribe.

The leader feels deeply but channels emotion into clarity, not reaction. Anger becomes boundary. Fear becomes focus. Doubt becomes humility.

The Currency of Consistency

Charisma attracts attention, but consistency earns allegiance.

When they can predict your standard, they relax into it. When they cannot, they prepare for impact.

Consistency is quiet power.

The Law of Credibility

Credibility rests on competence, character, and composure.

Competence proves you can. Character proves you should. Composure proves you will, even under fire.

Authority is not given. It is verified daily through credibility.

Influence Without Title

Influence does not require permission. It requires proof.

A janitor can influence a CEO if his standard never slips. A private can influence a platoon if his courage never wavers.

Leadership belongs to whoever holds the highest standard under pressure.

That is why true leaders often rise quietly. They perform at a level that forces others to adjust upward.

The Respect Cycle

Model what you expect. Maintain what you model. Magnify others who do the same.

Silence as a Weapon

Words lose value when overused. The leader speaks last and least, but when he does, the room listens. It gives men room to reveal themselves.

Use silence as a scalpel, not a shield.

Or keep talking and prove nothing.

Section 3: The Shield and the Sword

Every man carries two tools: the shield and the sword. Most men misuse both.

One protects. The other enforces.

A man who cannot protect or assert cannot lead. A good man must be dangerous. Dangerous means capable and controlled.

The Shield: Strength That Protects

The shield is your restraint: your ability to absorb pressure without losing direction. Only the man who can strike has the right to forgive.

Silence becomes armor. Stillness becomes authority. Power contained is more intimidating than power displayed.

Leadership begins the moment someone feels safe in your shadow.

The Sword: Strength That Enforces

The sword is your conviction: your capacity to act when action is demanded.

Truth spoken when silence would be easier. Boundaries enforced when compromise would be cheaper. Protection through precision, not aggression.

Blunt men cause chaos. Timid men enable it.

To wield it well, a man must know when he is defending principle versus ego. The sword does not create peace. It enforces the conditions where peace can exist.

The Monster Leashed

Inside every strong man lives a monster. Most men fear it. The wise man trains it.

He does not deny it. He disciplines it. When danger comes, he does not need to summon rage. It is already trained, waiting, obedient.

A harmless man cannot protect anyone. And everyone around him feels it.

A good man chooses to keep his monster leashed until necessity calls. That restraint is what separates guardians from tyrants.

Peace through capability, not compliance.

The Code of Conflict

Never fight for ego. Pride buys long-term regret.

Never submit to fear. Fear feeds on untrained strength.

Never attack the weak. A sword drawn against the defenseless dishonors its wielder.

Never draw the sword without readiness to finish. Half-measures breed escalation.

When you hold both the shield and sword in balance, you carry peace and power simultaneously.

Mastery in Duality

Too soft, and you lose authority. Too hard, and you lose connection.

Leadership without compassion becomes tyranny. Compassion without discipline becomes chaos.

Fail either, and you fail both.

Section 4: Brotherhood and Legacy

A great man's influence does not end with his breath. Or it never existed.

It echoes through those he strengthens.

Leadership without succession is performance. Leadership that multiplies itself becomes legacy.

The man of The Code measures leadership by how many men he makes capable of standing alone.

The Leader as Builder of Men

The mission stops being about his success and becomes about their strength.

Weak men build fans. Great men build brothers.

You start asking: Who can I raise to lead beside me? Who can I sharpen so they outgrow me?

True legacy is when your standard survives your absence.

If it doesn't, you were the system.

The highest form of leadership is replication.

The Brotherhood Principle

Brotherhood does not weaken independence. It amplifies it through alignment.

A strong circle does not flatter. It forges. It tells you when you are drifting. It calls you out without tearing you down. It celebrates discipline over talent.

Weak leaders need followers to feel powerful. Strong leaders want equals to feel challenged.

Iron sharpens iron, but only if both blades are willing to be scraped.

They sat across from each other, both knowing the conversation was not optional. No anger. No performance. Just truth.

"You're slipping."

He looked down before answering. No one else spoke.

No defense came back. Because it was true.

Not loyalty. Precision.

Weak men protect feelings. Brothers protect standards.

Brotherhood also requires vulnerability: the courage to admit fatigue without surrendering strength.

Family as the First Circle

The home is a leader's most honest battlefield. Your family does not see your performance. They see your patterns.

A father's greatest gift is modeling calm authority: showing his sons how to carry strength with patience and his daughters what a steady man looks like.

Your children will imitate your values, not your speeches.

The Culture of Standard

Legacy is a culture that outlives charisma. Legacy is what continues when you are no longer present.

Every decision you make, every standard you uphold, becomes brick-work in that culture. When your men start correcting each other by your example, you have crossed from leadership into legacy.

Culture does not require constant supervision. It requires clarity.

Set the standard high. Explain it once. Live it daily.

If it doesn't, it dies with you.

The Law of Multiplication

You lose nothing by strengthening others.

Give men a model of composure they can borrow until it becomes their own.

The Leader's Oath

"I will build men stronger than myself. I will sharpen without envy and correct without pride. I will protect the standard more than I protect my ego. And I will measure my leadership by what survives my absence."

Authority is never declared. It is observed.

Men do not follow titles. They follow standards.

If your authority depends on presence, it is fragile.

If it survives your absence, it is real.

Reflection

If I vanished, would my standard remain in the men I led?

LAW IV — LEGACY

Legacy

You multiply strength in others.

What you build in others continues when you are gone.

If it dies with you, you did not build it.

CHAPTER 5

THE FOUNDATION OF PRESENCE

Section 1: The Man Who Becomes His Code

A man reaches a point where discipline stops being effort and becomes identity. You are not there yet.

He does not need to think about doing what is right because it is no longer separate from who he is. In the beginning, every man needs structure to guide him: rituals, lists, laws, discipline. But the point of structure is not dependence. It is integration.

The rituals that once restrained him now express him. Discipline is no longer remembered. It is default.

The Dissolving of Ego

When a man becomes his Code, ego dissolves. He no longer compares. He no longer competes for validation. He is aligned with something deeper than image.

Some days it feels clean. Some days it feels lonely. He keeps moving anyway. He measures himself only against yesterday's version.

The man who stops reinforcing his Code does not return to where he started. He falls further. Because now the failure is conscious.

Because now he knows the law, and drift becomes a choice.

Your past self would not recognize your stillness.

Or it never becomes you.

Section 2: The Measure of a Life

Every man lives as if he has all the time in the world. You spend it like it won't run out.

Until time reminds him that he does not.

Mortality burns away vanity, noise, and distraction. It shows you what matters when the countdown becomes visible.

Mortality as Mirror

When time is finite, proving, posturing, and pleasing disappear. You begin to build only what is worth standing after you are gone.

There are only a limited number of sunrises left.

Waste enough of them, and regret becomes the final witness.

The Three Measures of Legacy: Impact, Integrity, Intimacy

1. Impact: What You Built

What did your strength create? Did your discipline become structure, your order become opportunity, your mission become meaning for others? It is the mark your actions left on your family, your craft, and your brothers.

2. Integrity: How You Built It

The man of The Code judges success not by size, but by source. How did you earn what you have? Whose trust paid the price for your progress? When methods match morals, legacy holds.

3. Intimacy: Who You Stayed Human For

Intimacy is not softness. It is stewardship. It is keeping your heart open enough to love deeply while still standing firm.

When you die, the world will forget your earnings, but your children will never forget how they felt around you.

Death as Audit, Not Enemy

Death asks: Did you build what mattered? Did you become who you said you would be?

You will think about consistency. Did your actions match your Code? Did you leave order or confusion behind?

The man who has lived by principle will not fear this audit.

I have had days where that thought hit me harder than any fear of dying ever did. He knows his measure will not be counted in years, but in alignment: how closely his life mirrored his principles when no one was watching.

If not, it ends unfinished.

Section 3: The Transfer of Fire

No man keeps the fire forever. He only tends it long enough to pass it on. Or he lets it die with him.

When your time ends, the question is simple: did you build others or only yourself?

The Fire as Knowledge

Your life's experience, the failures, the scars, the discipline, is all fuel meant to kindle others. When you share your fire, you shorten another man's learning curve. You make his path straighter, his burden lighter, his purpose clearer.

Mentorship as Legacy

He teaches best by living well. When others observe how he handles fatigue, failure, or success, they absorb his standards.

That is why composure is contagious.

It is handing them the map without dragging them up the mountain.

The Generational Torch

Every generation inherits a fire from the last. Sometimes bright. Sometimes dim.

Your job is to make it burn cleaner, steadier, stronger. That is why you raise sons with principle, not indulgence. That is why you teach daughters discernment through example, not fear. That is why you mentor younger men without envy, so the chain remains unbroken.

He designs his legacy so the next one must surpass him.

The Written Flame

If your lessons matter, preserve them. Write letters to your children, even if they are still too young to read them.

Some truths land better on paper than they ever do out loud.

Record what you learned the hard way so they can learn it the honorable way.

Words become a torch when the man who wrote them is gone.

Guarding the Flame

You must discern who is ready. Who is willing to respect what you hand them.

Do not waste energy preaching to ears closed by arrogance. Focus on the few who prove they are ready to carry it forward.

Teach only those who have proven they can protect what you built.

The Circle of Continuity

The man builds. The builder leads. The leader builds the next.

If you don't pass it, it ends here.

Section 4: Peace and Completion

After years of battle, striving, and building, the man of The Code arrives at a rare place. Most never reach it.

You already know how far you still are from it.

The Quiet Reward

There will come mornings when you wake up, and your own silence feels sacred. No guilt. No scrambling. The house stands because the ground is solid.

Forgiveness as Final Discipline

Forgiveness is the final act of control: releasing what no longer serves the mission.

Or carrying it until it poisons everything else.

Forgive the ones who misunderstood you. Forgive the ones who failed you. Forgive the man you used to be.

Not to excuse them. To stop dragging them forward.

Let the scars remain, but remove the poison beneath them.

When you realize the journey was never about conquest, peace stops feeling like surrender.

Or you never leave the shore.

And you call that peace.

Section 5: Mortality Gives Meaning

Mortality forces urgency into purpose. You've been delaying anyway.

The man of The Code uses death as a constraint. The reminder that today matters because it will never return.

Discipline builds the man.

Mortality decides what mattered.

The clock does not care what you intended.

It only counts what you did.

And it is already counting against you.

Reflection

What am I still carrying that no longer serves my life?

LAW V — MORTALITY

Mortality

You act with urgency because time is finite.

Time is what makes mastery count.

You are running out of it.

CHAPTER 6
THE CODE

Section 1: The Fifth Dawn

The Forge has gone cold. The hammer rests on the anvil. The scars on his hands are no longer reminders of failure. They are proof of refinement.

He rises before the sun. Not because he has to, but because that is who he is now. The world is still dark outside, and he welcomes it.

He does not announce it. He lives it.

Most men wait for a reason.

Remove it. Or stay where you are.

Section 2: The Laws in Motion

The laws no longer sit outside him as principles. They live inside him as identity. Yours are still optional.

LAW I — DISCIPLINE

Discipline forged me.

LAW II — ORDER

Order directed me.

LAW III — AUTHORITY

Authority refined me.

LAW IV — LEGACY

Legacy extended me.

LAW V — MORTALITY

Mortality measured me.

Lose one, and something collapses. Not later. Immediately. You've felt it happen.

Section 3: The Code as Compass

A man who carries his Code has direction wherever he stands. You can strip him of comfort, routine, even reputation, and he will still find his center.

Because The Code lives inside him now.

The compass does not point toward comfort. It points toward truth. You already know which one you follow.

When confusion hits, when emotion blurs logic, when temptation whispers, the man of The Code does not ask what feels right.

He asks what aligns with his law.

Even a true compass needs recalibration.

A man drifts. Slowly. Quietly. Through distraction and fatigue.

Drift long enough, and you stop noticing it. Until it costs you something you cannot rebuild. Until the gap costs you something you cannot get back.

That is why he builds ritual. A structure that realigns him before drift becomes distance.

His morning is not chaos. It is set.

The Silence Between Choices

The modern world worships noise.

He does not.

When others rush to speak, he waits. When others panic, he breathes. When others break formation, he holds.

Miss that moment, and you don't.

Section 4: The Oath of Iron

He stands where it started. His reflection glows in the dark iron, older now. He came here years ago to rebuild.

He no longer needs the heat. You still avoid it.

The fire moved inside him.

The Oath of Iron

"I am the keeper of my word.

I do not wait for strength. I build it.

I do not ask for peace. I earn it.

Discipline is my foundation.

Order is my direction.

Authority is my posture.

Legacy is my purpose.

Mortality is my reminder.

I am not the man I was.

I am the man I decided to become."

He lets the silence close around the words.

They do not echo.

They land.

He breathes once. Deep. Slow. Final. Then folds the paper.

He no longer speaks about discipline. It is seen in how he moves.

Slow. Certain. Unwasted.

The younger men watch him without asking questions. Not because he demands respect.

Because nothing in him needs it.

Section 5: The Dawn Beyond the Door

The Forge stands quiet behind him.

He does not look back.

He does not need to.

Ahead lies the world. Loud. Unstable. Unpredictable.

He no longer searches. You still are.

He acts.

The door is behind him.

The fire remains.

He walks.

You see it in what he no longer negotiates. And in what you still do.

You feel it in what no longer moves him.

And in what still controls you.

And long after he is gone,

you remember the standard he refused to lower.

Or you won't.

And nothing you built will last.

AWAKENING

Afghanistan was sand, silence, and waiting. Dust in his teeth. The same sky every day.

The world had told him war made men.

That clarity was found under fire.

Instead, he found it under fluorescent lights, repetition, and the hum of generators that never stopped.

Days blurred.

Same meals. Same patrols. Same conversations that went nowhere.

He started noticing it.

Not just there.

Everywhere.

Men breathing.

Existing.

Not living.

You've seen it.

He saw it in their eyes: survival mistaken for purpose.

One night, sitting outside the tent, the hum pressing into everything, it landed clean:

If I come home the same man who left, I wasted this.

He didn't want to be remembered for enduring.

He wanted to become someone who built.

The next morning, he wrote three words in a notebook:

No more wasting.

And this time, he meant it.

When he came home, he removed everything that made drift easy.

The Xbox went into the trash.

Noise went quiet.

He stopped waiting.

He started moving.

Every day, the same decision.

Again.

And again.

And again.

He lived like he was still deployed.

Focused.

Alert.

Accountable.

Only now, the mission was himself.

There was no exit this time.

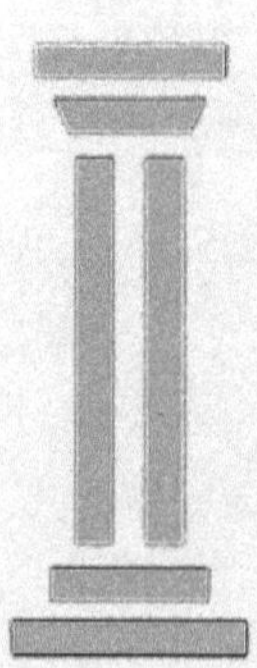

BOOK II
THE HOUSE

PEACE IS NOT THE ABSENCE OF NOISE, IT IS THE PRESENCE OF ORDER.

THE MAN BUILDS HIS WALLS NOT TO HIDE, BUT TO PROTECT WHAT IS SACRED WITHIN THEM.

CHAPTER 7

THE LAW OF THE ARENA

Section 1: The World as Arena

The moment a man steps beyond solitude, the world tests him. Every glance, challenge, delay, and betrayal demands proof.

No one cares what you claim. Only what you execute when conditions turn against you.

A man who cannot govern himself cannot be trusted with anything that matters.

You are always being measured.

Not by others.

By consequence.

And consequence does not forget. It collects.

The End of Theory

The Field builds. The Arena tests.

It is easy to sound disciplined in silence. Harder when insulted, ignored, or betrayed.

Easy to claim morality when untested. Harder when comfort tempts and fear presses.

Every decision exposes it.

Adversity verifies.

The trial repeats until you pass with composure.

Not aggression. Not avoidance.

Composure.

The Law of The Arena

The Arena divides men.

Those who wait for conditions.

And those who prepare for resistance.

The man of The Code prepares.

He does not expect fairness.

He expects friction.

Friction refines him. Ease dulls. Resistance sharpens.

You do not win through approval.

You win by maintaining order under pressure.

Or you react. And lose control.

The Distinction

The Field is where a man builds himself.

The Arena is where that build is tested.

In the Field, failure is contained.

In the Arena, failure has consequence.

In the Field, he repeats until it works.

In the Arena, it must work when it matters.

Confuse the two, and you train wrong.

Train wrong, and the Arena exposes it.

Section 2: The Difference Between Danger and Drama

The Arena tests a man through threat and through noise.

Some battles sharpen him.

Others drain him.

The distinction decides everything.

Most men confuse motion with progress and conflict with purpose.

They mistake drama for danger and spend their lives reacting to what cannot harm them.

The Drain of Distraction

Drama feeds on attention.

It grows with emotion and dies in silence.

The modern man is surrounded by it.

Opinions. Arguments. Headlines. Provocation.

I have burned hours in arguments that changed nothing.

Same problems.

Just louder.

That is the cost.

Time you do not get back. And nothing to show for it.

It is smoke.

Chase it long enough and you forget what fire even looks like.

Real danger does not announce itself.

It moves quietly.

It ends things.

Peace. Mission. Life.

The man of The Code saves his fire for that.

He does not spend it on noise, debate, or ego.

The Rule of Response

Drama wants reaction.

Danger requires response.

When his pulse rises, he asks:

Is this a threat or a performance?

If it is performance, he disengages.

If it is threat, he moves.

He moves with precision.

Emotion follows later.

His focus stays owned.

When Danger Arrives

When real danger comes, he moves.

Not loud. Not emotional.

Precise.

Training replaces thought. Breath slows. Action simplifies.

He does not attack blindly.

He solves.

Danger exposes the truth.

Whether composure is practiced or performed.

He does what is required.

He protects what is his.

Then he returns to stillness.

A warrior fights when necessary.

A fool fights constantly.

The enemy is not always in front of him.

And if you don't control it, it controls everything else.

Section 3: Building Competitive Calm

Pressure does not build character. It exposes yours.

It reveals what you built when no one was watching.

In The Arena, composure is not luxury.

It is survival.

The man of The Code does not aim to feel comfortable under pressure.

He aims to remain effective.

Because when he fails here, something real pays for it. And it's usually not just him.

Breath as Anchor

The first weapon of composure is breath.

When panic rises, physiology follows.

Heart rate spikes. Focus narrows. Decisions degrade.

The man who controls breath controls biology.

He trains it deliberately.

Before arguments.

Before competition.

Before action.

Slow inhale.

Controlled exhale.

Breath is the manual override.

The first time it works, everything slows.

Not because the situation changed.

Because he did.

Preparation as Peace

Calm is not found in the moment.

It is built long before it is needed.

Preparation turns chaos into something familiar.

That is built in the Field. It is proven in the Arena.

When others freeze, he moves.

Not because he is fearless.

Because he has seen this before.

This is why he trains beyond comfort.

He chases proof.

Repetition is the parent of calm.

Focus as Firebreak

When pressure peaks, the world tries to fragment attention.

The man of The Code cuts it down.

One problem.

One decision.

One execution.

Focus breaks panic into steps.

That is the difference.

Anyone can look strong when things go right.

Only the composed stay strong when everything goes wrong.

The Arena respects neither size nor speed.

Only steadiness.

When the world grows loud again, he does not answer it.

He moves through it.

Clean.

Because calm is not a personality.

Or you don't have it when it matters.

Section 4: Turning Failure Into Data

Failure used to feel like death. You still react like it is.

Now it feels like instruction.

That is the difference between the man who stays broken and the man who builds.

Both fall.

The Arena does not excuse mistakes.

It records them.

And the man who reads that record improves.

Failure as a Feedback Loop

Every setback becomes an audit.

Not a wound.

Step One. Replay.

Walk through the event without drama.

What happened?

What did you expect?

What was under your control?

Step Two. Extract.

What pattern caused the break?

Discipline. Decision. Direction.

Step Three. Apply.

Change behavior immediately.

Turn data into correction before memory dulls.

Failure is worthless without implementation.

Delay is decay.

Falling Forward

Every man will fall in The Arena.

But falling forward means failing with momentum.

The untrained man stops after falling.

The trained man adjusts.

He collects each mistake.

Not as regret.

As material.

He rebuilds with it.

Every broken piece becomes part of something stronger.

He does not dramatize the fall.

He converts it.

The Long Game of Refinement

Each loss teaches him where discipline meets limitation.

Each mistake defines the edges of his current mastery.

Over time, he begins to seek friction.

Not pain.

Precision.

He does not chase perfection.

He sharpens accuracy.

He documents what he learns.

Not for comfort.

For correction.

Because in The Arena, the man who wins is not the one who never falls.

Or you stay down.

And that becomes your pattern.

Section 5: The Night Audit

Every day in The Field ends the same way.

In silence.

Not the absence of sound.

The absence of excuse.

The man stands alone again, as he did in The Forge.

But now the silence is not for rebuilding.

It is for review.

No audience.

No justification.

No escape.

The day tested him.

Every moment showed him something.

Where he held.

Where he slipped.

And what it cost him.

It always costs more than you admit.

Reflection

Where did I act with clarity?

Where did emotion override order?

Where did I protect peace?

Where did I betray my standard?

CHAPTER 8

THE MAN IN STILLNESS

Section 1: The House as Proof

I learned that the hard way. I could hold composure outside and still walk into a house that felt off the moment I stepped in.

That disconnect costs more than you think. You've felt it walking in.

Before a man leads the world, he must command the four walls that hold his peace.

A home reflects the man who maintains it. Chaos rarely starts outside. It leaks outward from what you have not handled.

The standard you tolerate becomes the structure you are forced to live in.

He does not organize his home to impress.

He does it because without it, he drifts.

Every system maintained reinforces order within.

Governance is not control.

It is rhythm.

Structure removes friction and protects focus.

Everything has a place. Everything has a time. Everything has a standard.

Because structure absorbs pressure.

Without it, stress becomes chaos.

With it, disruption is contained.

Peace built on circumstance is fragile.

Peace built on discipline holds.

Order is not enforced once.

It is enforced daily.

The First Law of The House — Order

"I will keep my home clean because it mirrors my mind.

I will set rhythm where disorder forms.

I will govern my environment as proof of discipline.

My home will be my first kingdom.

Order will be its law."

A man's home is not retreat.

Or it exposes you.

Section 2: The Anchor of Family

He is not the loudest voice in the room.

He is the weight that keeps the room from drifting.

Your children will not remember most of what you say.

They will repeat how you lived.

And they will pay for where you were inconsistent.

His family does not need perfection.

They need him stable. Not when it's easy.

There were nights I wanted to correct everything at once.

Tone sharp. Energy off.

That never built anything.

Protection is more than defense from harm.

It is the prevention of chaos.

He cannot shield his family from every storm.

But he can make sure he is not one of them.

He absorbs pressure first.

So it does not spill onto them. When it does, it's yours. And they live inside it.

That is the cost of being the anchor.

Promises mean nothing if they are unpredictable.

Children do not measure him by what he says.

They measure him by how consistent his peace is.

Children do not follow rules.

They copy patterns.

Everyone brings their tides.

Stress. Fear. Exhaustion. Hope.

He does not fix every problem.

He gives structure to emotion so it does not flood the house.

He does not demand obedience.

He earns alignment.

If he needs to control everything, he has already lost control of himself.

What they carry will not be his words.

It will be his rhythm.

The Second Law of The House — Presence

"I will protect through presence, not pressure.

I will lead through rhythm, not reaction.

I will be the still point my family can rely on.

My calm will become their inheritance."

It is built through thousands of small acts.

He came home late, still carrying the day in his shoulders.

The house was loud.

Toys out. Dishes in the sink. Voices layered.

He felt the urge to correct everything at once.

Instead, he set his keys down quietly.

Picked up one plate.

Then another.

The room shifted.

Not because he demanded it.

Because he demonstrated it.

The house does not rise to your expectations.

It settles into your behavior.

Section 3: The Partnership Code

He sees what needs to be done.

She feels what he misses.

When both are respected, decisions sharpen.

When either is dismissed, the structure weakens.

Leadership in partnership is clarity. You've made it control before.

Not control.

Most conflict is not disagreement.

It is tone. Timing. Ego.

The man who leads with calm invites cooperation.

The man who leads with ego creates resistance.

And pays for it later. Always.

Every strong partnership endures conflict.

But the great man does not compete with the person he loves.

He competes with his own impatience.

If he wins the argument but loses the connection,

he lost.

Attraction survives on polarity.

Respect sustains it.

Some seasons require his structure to lead.

Others require her awareness to stabilize.

When she softens, he protects.

When she strengthens, he supports.

When she doubts, he steadies.

When he drifts, she reflects it.

Or ego breaks it.

Not dominance.

The Third Law of The House — Partnership

"I will lead with clarity, not control.

I will hold the frame without silencing the feminine.

I will build equilibrium, not competition.

My love will be disciplined, and my discipline will be loving."

Section 4: The Fortress of Peace

The home must become a fortress of peace.

Peace is not found.

It is built.

And it is defended.

If you do not defend your peace,

someone else will define it.

He limits the entry points.

Too many voices.

Too much noise.

Too many screens.

I have felt the shift the moment noise returns.

Calm disappears faster than it was built. Because you let it.

That is the cost.

Morning: silence before the day's noise.

Evening: reflection before rest.

Weekly: shared meals, real conversation, gratitude spoken.

These are not habits.

They are safeguards.

Tone as Atmosphere

When his presence enters, the temperature shifts.

When his composure holds, the house stabilizes.

Or it doesn't.

And that exposes him.

The Fourth Law of The House — Peace

"I will defend the silence within my walls.

I will build peace through boundaries and ritual.

My tone will set the weather of this house.

Or nothing will."

Section 5: The Oath of Home

The home is quiet now.

Not perfect.

Stable.

He walks through it and notices immediately.

What used to feel forced now feels natural.

That is the difference.

He understands now his home is not a possession.

It is a responsibility.

He is its keeper.

Not its ruler.

He does not guard it for power.

He guards it for peace.

The Oath of Home

"I will keep my home clean in spirit and in space.

I will protect its silence from the noise of the world.

I will love through consistency, not condition.

I will treat every room as reflection, every moment as memory.

I will guard the peace I have built, and let no chaos take it."

Because if he does not hold that line, it breaks.

No one else will.

The home is not his retreat.

And if it's not, that's on you.

CHAPTER 9

THE OATH OF THE HOUSE

Section 1: The Law of Tolerance

Peace that is not enforced becomes disorder.

A house is never neutral.

It is held together by standard or pulled apart by what is tolerated.

Every repeated behavior leaves an imprint. It settles. It lingers. Then it becomes atmosphere. And atmosphere becomes law.

The man of The Code does not wait.

What is allowed quietly will rule loudly. You let it happen.

The Invisible Architecture

A house is not defined by walls. It is defined by what repeats inside them.

Conversation. Tone. Care. Behavior left uncorrected.

These are the beams.

If they weaken, the structure follows.

Disorder does not begin with collapse. It begins with permission.

A towel left once becomes a pile. A tone unchecked becomes habit.

Nothing stays small.

What repeats becomes normal. What becomes normal becomes culture. Culture decides whether The House holds or erodes.

What a Man Permits

The condition of a house is not accidental. It is permitted.

Noise without direction. Tension without correction. Drift without interruption.

All of it enters through inaction.

Leadership is not proven in what a man values. It is proven in what he allows to continue.

What you tolerate trains The House.

The House does not respond to intention. It responds to repetition.

And repetition answers to standard.

Disorder rarely enters as chaos. It enters as convenience.

A moment not corrected. A standard softened. A line ignored.

Each one teaches The House what is acceptable.

Over time, the unacceptable becomes expected.

Delay is permission. And you've delayed before.

The man who avoids small corrections inherits large problems.

And he will call them unfair because he failed to call them early.

Peace Is Built

Peace is not the absence of conflict. It is the result of structure.

A house feels calm because problems are handled cleanly.

Not avoided.

Resolved.

The man does not chase peace. He builds it.

He removes what disrupts it. Reinforces what sustains it. Maintains it daily.

Quietly. Without announcement.

At some point, the man stops reacting. He decides.

What is allowed. What is corrected. What is not tolerated.

Not through words.

Through consistency.

The House does not need explanation.

It needs stability.

When the standard is lived, alignment follows.

Not from fear.

From clarity.

If the standard is low, disorder becomes normal. If the standard is clear, order becomes automatic.

He defines the outcome.

Then he holds the line.

The Audit of The House

A man who wants truth does not ask how he feels. He looks at what repeats.

Tone. Condition. Respect. Conflict. Discipline.

These are evidence.

If disorder repeats, it is permitted. If tension lingers, it is avoided. If disrespect appears, it was not corrected.

There was a time I walked into my own place and felt tension before anyone spoke.

Nothing was said.

But I knew something was off.

That was my standard slipping.

Not theirs.

The House reflects what is enforced and exposes what is ignored.

Nothing inside his house exists without his permission.

Not because he controls everyone.

Because he sets the standard.

If The House is calm, he built it.

If it is unstable, he allowed it.

There is no one else to blame.

Section 2: What The House Allows

The House is defined by what it permits to live and repeat inside it. That includes yours.

Not everything is removed.

Some things are protected.

Restriction alone creates rigidity. Structured allowance creates stability.

Emotion

Emotion is allowed.

Frustration. Fatigue. Doubt. Anger.

It can rise.

It just cannot take control.

He does not punish emotion. He contains it.

It can exist.

It does not govern.

No shouting that breaks the frame. No silence that corrodes connection. No reaction that replaces responsibility.

Imperfection

Mistakes are allowed.

Failure. Forgetting. Falling short.

Perfection is not the standard.

Correction is.

Mistakes are handled cleanly. Named. Adjusted. Finished.

Not carried.

Not weaponized.

Rest

Rest is allowed.

Stillness. Silence. Recovery.

The home is not another arena.

Exhaustion breeds instability.

Rest restores structure.

Truth

Truth is allowed.

Especially when it is uncomfortable.

He builds a house where truth can be spoken without destroying connection.

Truth without ego. Correction without attack. Listening without defense.

Clean.

Direct.

Finished.

Growth

Growth is allowed.

No one is fixed. No one is finished.

But growth is directed.

Measured against the standard.

Growth without direction becomes drift. Drift becomes decay. Decay becomes normal.

Every allowance teaches The House how to behave.

So he reinforces what builds order.

Emotion expressed cleanly is reinforced. Truth spoken with discipline is reinforced. Rest that restores structure is reinforced. Growth aligned with the standard is reinforced.

What is rewarded becomes stronger. Whether you meant to reward it or not.

What becomes stronger defines The House.

A strong house is not silent.

It is structured.

Or it erodes. And you let it.

Section 3: What The House Rejects

A house that allows everything becomes ruled by anything.

Peace is protected by what is refused. You've refused less than you should.

Disrespect

Disrespect is corrected early.

Not emotionally.

Immediately.

Without hesitation.

What is not corrected becomes standard.

If respect is optional, it disappears.

Chronic Disorder

Disorder is not the mess.

It is the lack of correction.

The man corrects before disorder becomes identity.

Early correction prevents structural decay.

Passive Decay

The most dangerous threats are absences.

Avoided conversations. Unspoken tension. Growing distance.

He addresses drift early.

Before distance becomes silence.

Before silence becomes separation.

Because what is ignored compounds. And it always returns larger.

Emotional Chaos

Emotion is allowed.

Chaos is not.

He contains escalation. He removes instability from the environment.

Because chaos normalized destroys peace.

Excuses

Excuses do not exist.

Explanation may exist.

Accountability must follow.

Patterns that do not change are corrected.

Words do not reset the standard.
Behavior does.

Inconsistency

Inconsistency destroys authority.

Standards do not shift with mood. They do not disappear under pressure.

Without consistency, everything becomes negotiable.

And negotiation is where standards die.

The Cost of Tolerance

Every house has a structural limit.

He does not find it.

He protects it.

Because once instability begins, correction becomes harder.

So he acts early.

Quietly.

Cleanly.

A man who delays correction is not keeping peace.

And he will pay it.

Section 4: The Discipline of Correction

A standard not enforced is a suggestion. That's how yours have been treated.

Correction is where leadership becomes visible.

Timing

Correction is immediate.

Delay multiplies resistance. It weakens authority.

Delivery

Correction is calm.

Emotion distorts clarity.

Structure

One correction. One standard. One reset.

No lectures. No history.

Placement

Private when it preserves dignity.

Public when it protects structure.

Follow Through

Correction without enforcement is theater. And everyone sees it.

Behavior decides outcome.

Finality

Correction ends clean.

No emotional residue. No revisiting. No dragging it forward.

Consistency becomes authority.

Until then, you don't have it.

Section 5: The Oath of The House

The House is quiet.

Not from avoidance.

From order.

Nothing feels tense because nothing is unclear.

You remember when everything felt tense and no one said why.

That confusion is gone now.

There comes a point where the man stops negotiating.

The line becomes fixed. Yours hasn't been.

Everything organizes around it.

Correction is no longer something he does.

It is something he is.

He sees deviation.

He corrects.

Clean. Immediate. Finished.

The Oath of The House

"I will correct immediately, not emotionally.

I will enforce the standard without apology.

I will not delay what must be addressed.

I will not soften truth to avoid tension.

If the line is crossed, I will restore it.

Starting with myself."

The man who corrects early never has to fight late.

The one who delays always does.

Because every house eventually obeys one thing:

the standard enforced most consistently.

If your house is unstable,

you allowed it.

Reflection

If my home is stable, my life is aligned.
The home is not his retreat.

CHAPTER 10

THE LAW OF POLARITY

Section 1: The Polarity Principle

When a man loses direction, the relationship begins to drift.

Masculinity and femininity are not enemies. They are patterns: archetypal tendencies, not rigid rules.

Complements under pressure.

Polarity is not competition.

Emotion tests the frame.

It does not define it.

The masculine provides direction and containment. The feminine provides movement and amplification.

The Design of Polarity

Polarity is the tension that creates attraction, order, and growth.

Masculine energy moves outward: build, protect, decide.

Feminine energy moves inward: nurture, express, renew.

Modern life pressures men to soften and women to harden.

That does not create harmony.

It creates confusion.

When direction disappears, tension replaces attraction.

Equality is not sameness. It is equal dignity expressed through different responsibilities.

Direction and Amplification

The masculine leads with clarity through conduct.

The feminine amplifies the quality of that conduct.

If he leads with chaos, chaos expands.

If he leads with order, peace expands.

A woman does not respond to his speeches.

She responds to his nervous system.

The feminine does not follow words.

It follows stability.

If his direction is unstable, her energy becomes restless.

If his frame is steady, her nature relaxes.

The Collapse of Polarity

When men lose direction, women are forced to compensate.

They take control because the frame is absent.

And though they appear strong, the dynamic becomes unsustainable: pressure without containment.

A woman may carry the weight for a season.

But she will not desire the man who made her carry his.

Restoring the Dance

Restoring polarity is not domination.

It is a return to design.

Masculine leadership is containment: the ability to hold emotion, uncertainty, and pressure without losing posture.

Femininity yields when trust exists, not when fear is applied.

When a man embodies direction, the feminine relaxes.

When he drifts, the relationship becomes negotiation instead of creation.

Containment is not restriction.

It is safety.

The Polarity Code

A man does not demand trust he has not earned through steadiness.

A man does not call instability leadership.

A man holds direction instead of reacting to emotion.

If his posture collapses, respect leaves with it.

Polarity does not respond to intention.

It responds to frame.

The man who holds direction gives freedom.

The woman who receives direction gives beauty.

Or they don't. And it turns into resentment.

Section 2: The Calm and the Current

The feminine is movement.

The masculine is containment.

Between them, life breathes.

She is change, emotion, current.

He is the frame that keeps the current from becoming a flood.

When the frame holds, the relationship flows.

When it fails, chaos enters.

The Nature of the Feminine

The feminine is chaos only to the untrained man.

To the wise, she is rhythm: deeper than logic, wider than reason.

Her emotions move like weather.

Not random.

Responsive.

She speaks in tone, silence, and shift.

One question sits beneath it:

Can you hold the relationship steady without collapsing into reaction or retreat?

The Role of the Masculine

The man's duty in this dynamic is not to suppress her emotion.

It is to absorb it without distortion.

He does not mirror her chaos.

He contains it.

Not through dominance or retreat, but through anchored energy: breath slow, tone steady, eyes clear.

Calm is not apathy.

It is disciplined presence.

A woman will only rest inside a man who can remain centered while she is changing.

That is the paradox.

Her movement requires his stillness.

But his stillness must be alive, not cold.

He must hold, not cage.

Guide, not silence.

When Calm Turns Into Distance

Some men call shutdown composure.

It is not.

True calm is engaged stillness: listening without losing ground.

If your calm creates disconnection, it is avoidance.

If your silence feels cold, it is not strength.

It is fear dressed as control.

The masculine role is to channel emotion, not mute it.

When she rages, lower your tone, not your standard.

When she doubts, offer direction, not debate.

When she fears, provide certainty, not defense.

If your frame depends on her mood, it is not a frame. It's weakness you renamed.

The Discipline of Emotional Alchemy

Masculine calm is not natural.

It is trained.

It is built through repetition, friction, and reflection.

He learns not to react to emotion but to translate it.

He recognizes patterns instead of taking storms personally.

When she is upset, he does not see accusation.

He sees pressure testing the vessel.

If the frame bends, he repairs it.

If it holds, he reinforces it.

That is how love becomes respect.

Because the woman does not need perfection.

She needs containment.

The ability to remain unshaken under waves of feeling.

The storm respects only what stays standing.

Every time he passes her tests, trust deepens.

A woman drawn to masculine strength does not want control.

She wants containment.

When you become emotionally reactive, the frame cracks.

When the frame holds, trust grows.

The Containment Creed

When emotion rises, the man anchors instead of escalating.

His calm is engaged, not avoidant.

His presence softens tension rather than amplifying it.

When pressure increases, his spine strengthens.

Containment is not suppression.

It is steadiness under current.

The dynamic reveals the man.

Her movement gives him something to measure his strength against.

And when he learns to hold her current without drowning in it, he becomes what few men ever become: a sanctuary.

The calm man is not unfeeling.

Or he isn't. And she feels it immediately.

Section 3: The Protector's Burden

Protection is not about power. You've confused it before.

It is about responsibility.

A weak man seeks to control.

A strong man seeks to protect.

The man of The Code understands that his strength is not for himself.

It is for the order he creates around him: his home, his woman, his mission, his peace.

The Three Fronts of Protection

Protection has three fronts:

1. Physical — capability.

You build a body that can defend. You avoid fights, but you are not harmless.

2. Emotional — regulation.

Your stress does not become her instability. Your anger does not become the atmosphere.

3. Moral — leadership.

You guard the tone, the values, and the standards that govern The House.

A protector does not shield her from life.

He steadies the structure while life hits it.

Guarding Without Controlling

Protection becomes poison when it crosses into possession.

The line between guardianship and control is drawn by trust.

Control says, "Do as I say because I fear losing you."

Protection says, "I lead because I refuse to let chaos consume us."

A controlling man moves from insecurity.

A protecting man moves from clarity.

He understands that freedom, not fear, is what keeps love alive.

You cannot protect what you do not respect.

His authority is not built on dominance.

It is built on discipline.

The more stable his foundation, the more willingly she follows his lead.

He does not have to prove power.

His steadiness proves it for him.

The Weight of Provision

Protection extends beyond safety.

It includes provision.

Provision is not just money.

It is creating stability, direction, and opportunity.

He provides certainty: a vision for where they are going.

He provides order: systems that make chaos manageable.

He provides peace: a calm environment where she can express herself without fear.

A man who provides these becomes irreplaceable, not because of control, but because of contribution.

His presence adds structure.

His absence exposes it.

Provision is not payment.

It is stability delivered daily.

And if he cannot provide stability, he should stop confusing income with provision. Because she already knows the difference.

He carries pressure quietly so others do not fracture.

The Protector's Creed

The protector guards order, not ego.

He does not disguise insecurity as control.

His discipline defines the atmosphere of The House.

When pressure rises, his structure holds.

Protection is not dramatic.

It is reliable.

It is the silent promise that when the storm comes, he will still be standing.

Because peace is not the absence of threat.

It is the presence of a man who refuses to run.

A protector does not promise safety.

Or he doesn't. And everything starts to erode.

Section 4: The Weight of Leadership

Leadership is not a privilege. You've treated it like one.

It is a burden.

The man who seeks leadership for validation collapses under its weight.

The man who accepts it as duty becomes strong enough to carry it.

Masculine leadership is direction and containment.

You do not outsource stability to her emotions.

You do not negotiate your posture because the room is loud.

A leader listens without being moved.

He adjusts when truth demands it, not when pressure demands it.

He does not lead for agreement.

He leads for order.

If the relationship feels anxious, chaotic, or unstable, the frame is failing. And it's yours.

If it feels safe, calm, and clear, the frame is holding.

That is the measure: peace.

THE MAN WHO LET THE FRAME SLIP

Most men do not lose their authority in a single moment.

They surrender it in inches.

No one noticed when it began.

There was no fight.

No betrayal.

No slammed door.

Just small abdications.

He stopped deciding where they were going and began asking what she preferred.

Stopped setting standards and started negotiating them.

Stopped confronting tension and learned to smooth it over.

He called it peace.

It was drift.

At first she compensated naturally.

She chose the restaurant.

Managed the calendar.

Handled the conflict he felt but would not name.

He called her strong.

He did not see the fatigue gathering behind her eyes.

Weeks passed.

Then months.

He grew agreeable.

Careful.

Measured.

The arguments disappeared.

So did the charge.

At dinner one night she spoke quietly.

"I feel alone… even when you're here."

Not angry.

Certain.

He nodded.

Promised to be more present.

Bought flowers the next morning.

They sat on the table between them.

Bright.

Powerless.

After that, nothing collapsed.

It thinned.

She stopped bringing him her fears.

Stopped asking his opinion.

Stopped leaning her weight into him when something felt heavy.

The house grew quieter.

Not calm.

Airless.

He sensed it in small ways.

The pause before she answered him.

The way decisions no longer required him.

The way she carried herself without reaching.

One evening he reached for her hand.

She let him hold it.

Her fingers rested in his.

They did not close.

He lay awake beside her that night.

Close enough to feel her breathing.

Not heavy enough to change it.

Section 5: The Oath of Polarity

The man stands in stillness.

The world moves fast. Emotional. Loud.

He does not flinch.

His stillness is not distance.

It is direction.

He no longer argues to win.

He no longer performs strength.

He holds the frame. Or he loses it.

And in that frame, the feminine can relax without losing her fire.

The Stillness Oath

"I will lead through conduct, not control.

I will hold the frame when emotion rises.

I will not punish her with withdrawal.

I will not meet her current with chaos.

My calm will be engaged.

My direction will be clean.

I will be worthy of her trust.

My posture does not depend on her mood."

The Standard

Polarity is the result of a man who can hold pressure without collapsing into reaction or retreat.

If your frame is real, trust follows.

If your frame is false, resentment grows.

Because polarity does not lie.

It reveals the strength of the man holding it.

If your frame breaks under pressure,
this is where it ends.

Reflection

Where does my leadership disappear when stress rises?

Where do I control instead of contain?

Where do my actions contradict the trust I request?

CHAPTER 11

THE OATH OF ENDURANCE

Section 1: The Breaking Point

Every man meets a moment that splits his life into before and after. You already know yours.

It does not always come through violence or betrayal. It arrives as silence, as the sudden disappearance of certainty.

When the world he built goes silent, everything he trusted is tested.

When the woman he led turns away. When the brother he trusted speaks his name with venom. When the friend who vowed loyalty starts talking to the enemy.

It tightens the chest. Shortens the breath. Reality narrows.

The mind says, "This is not happening."

But it is.

And The Forge opens again.

The Collapse of Certainty

Betrayal does not just hurt because of what is lost. It hurts because it unmakes what you believed was true.

It is not the act that breaks you.

It is the realization that you were wrong about what you thought was solid.

Trust does not die loudly.

It collapses inward.

Betrayal exposes what you trusted without discipline.

And that exposure is where the pain gets honest.

THE NIGHT HE DIDN'T CALL

They had been brothers for over a decade.

The kind built in motion.

Late drives. Shared debts. The quiet understanding that if the world tilted, neither would stand alone.

There was no speech about loyalty.

There did not need to be.

When it matters, you call.

When you call, I come.

At 2:11 a.m., his phone lit the ceiling.

He was awake already.

The name on the screen tightened his chest.

He answered without greeting.

Breathing.

Then:

"I need you."

The voice was thinner than he had ever heard it.

"Where are you?"

An address.

Across town.

"I'm coming."

Boots.

Keys.

Door.

The engine turned before the fear finished forming.

Halfway there, the phone rang again.

He expected urgency.

He heard voices.

Not shouting.

Laughter.

Low. Contained.

"What's going on?"

"Nothing. Don't worry about it."

Wind pressed against the truck.

"You said you needed me."

"Yeah. I thought I did."

Another

"It's handled."

"You sure?"

"Yeah. Go back home."

The line went dead.

He kept driving another block before turning around.

The next morning he learned what happened from someone else.

There had been a confrontation.

Words sharp enough to cut.

A table overturned.

Men stepping forward.

Another man had stood where he would have stood.

Someone newer.

Someone easier to explain things to.

The realization did not explode.

It settled.

He replayed the sound of the laughter in the truck.

Soft.

Not meant for him.

He did not call to ask why.

He did not demand reassurance.

He watched.

Over the next weeks, the distance arranged itself.

Calls shorter.

Details filtered.

Plans made without him.

Nothing dramatic.

Just a quiet understanding that the rule between them no longer ran both directions.

Years later, when someone asked if they were still close, he answered simply.

"We were."

No bitterness.

No speech.

At 2:11 a.m., when the dark presses in and a name lights your ceiling, you find out whether you are history or still required.

The Anatomy of the Break

The breaking point does not come all at once.

First disbelief. Denial that this could happen.

Then rage. The ego fighting to reassert control.

Then silence.

Not peace.

Emptiness.

That silence is where most men quit.

They numb. They distract. They rebuild too fast.

But the man of The Code stays there.

He does not run.

He studies the fracture.

He wants to know exactly where it failed.

Not only who failed him.

Betrayal begins with others.

Correction begins with the self.

When the Fire Hits

At the moment of collapse, emotion is fire.

You cannot think clearly.

The mind spins, searching for explanation, for justice, for apology.

None of those bring relief.

The fire shows what still owns you emotionally.

It teaches you where you placed your peace in the hands of others.

That is why it burns so deeply.

It is not only about them.

It is about dependence being ripped from your hands.

Pain is the invoice for the peace you outsourced. And you signed it.

The Birth of Clarity

Every man must lose something he thought he could not live without to discover what he actually is.

You stop expecting rescue.

You stop waiting.

You begin to see that the fire did not come to destroy you.

It came to show you how much of you was still flammable.

The breaking point is not where you end.

It is where illusion does.

And when the smoke clears, the silence that terrified you starts to sound like peace.

Not comfort.

Clarity.

The kind that says:

Now you build without illusion. Or you repeat it.

The First Law of Betrayal — Misplaced Trust

Peace placed in undisciplined hands will return as pain.

Illusions survive only where correction stops.

History cannot replace alignment.

The break begins where truth stopped being spoken.

Section 2: The Silence After Fire

After the fire comes silence.

Not peace.

Silence.

Heavy.

The kind that makes the heart echo too loudly inside the chest.

Everything familiar has burned away.

The structure. The rhythm. The certainty.

One morning you realize no one is coming. You felt that already.

The calls stop. The noise fades.

The world keeps moving, but you have fallen still.

The Nature of the Void

This is where most men run.

The void is not emptiness.

It is what remains when distraction is removed and a man meets himself without noise.

They think the worst is over once the betrayal happens.

It is not.

The aftermath is worse.

The numbness that comes when anger loses its fuel and you are left with nothing to hold onto.

You will be tempted to fill it.

Noise. Women. Alcohol. Work. Distraction.

Anything to avoid feeling empty. And every escape made you weaker.

But that emptiness is not a flaw.

It is a furnace.

It is the space where your identity starts rebuilding itself without illusion.

If you can stand still long enough in the silence, the man who emerges will no longer need the things that burned.

Silence does not destroy the man.

It dissolves the mask.

You do not heal from betrayal by pretending it did not matter.

You heal by removing the need that made it possible.

When the Echo Turns Inward

In silence, the mind turns on itself.

Every regret, every mistake, every what if surfaces like a ghost.

It is natural to feel guilt for ignoring signs, for trusting the wrong people, for not seeing the blade before it cut.

But guilt only becomes useful when it turns into correction.

Otherwise, it becomes another room you rot inside.

The Gift Hidden in Isolation

The silence isolates you for a reason.

It forces you to hear your own thoughts without interference.

It strips away validation, sympathy, and applause until only truth remains.

Most men never reach this stage.

They escape too early.

But the man who stays learns something rare:

Solitude is not loneliness.

It is alignment.

The Discipline of Stillness

Stillness is not passive.

It is work.

To sit alone with pain and refuse to numb it, that is discipline.

To face the parts of yourself that contributed to your downfall, that is accountability.

To let emotion pass through without acting on it, that is mastery.

Every hour in silence reforges armor.

Not bravado.

Steel.

The kind that does not need to prove strength anymore because it is strength.

Stillness is where pain becomes precision.

The Shift

At some point, days, weeks, or months later, something subtle changes.

You stop replaying the betrayal.

You stop needing closure.

You stop waiting for the phone to ring.

The silence that once felt suffocating now feels spacious.

Your mind becomes clear, not empty.

You realize you no longer want to escape.

You want to build.

That is when you know the fire has done its work.

The new life is smaller.

Simpler.

But solid.

Or you haven't. And you're still hiding.

The Second Law of Betrayal — Silence

Silence does not abandon a man.

It exposes him.

Distraction delays refinement.

Stillness begins it.

The moment comes when a man stops running from his own reflection.

Section 3: Transmuting Pain to Power

What remains must now be used.

Pain is energy. You've wasted it before.

It burns, but it also fuels.

That is where transformation begins.

Not by escaping pain, but by harnessing it.

By turning chaos into motion, suffering into structure, heartbreak into hunger.

The Alchemy of Emotion

Most men treat pain as poison.

They try to suppress it, medicate it, or pretend it does not exist.

But pain, when faced correctly, is raw material.

Unrefined strength waiting for direction.

The process is alchemy:

Anger becomes focus.

Grief becomes clarity.

Shame becomes discipline.

Loneliness becomes solitude.

It is not instant.

It is deliberate.

Each emotion is examined, named, and repurposed.

What once broke you now becomes leverage.

You stop reacting to what hurt you and start building because of it.

The Power of Redirection

Pain that has nowhere to go becomes destruction.

And you've seen what it does when it turns on you.

Or it stays poison. And it keeps running your life.

That is why the man of The Code channels it through creation.

Lifting. Writing. Building. Leading. Mentoring.

He stops letting pain control his identity and starts letting it refine his habits.

Every rep in the gym becomes a meditation.

Every new skill becomes proof that the wound did not win.

Structure disciplines pain.

It transforms it.

When you convert emotion into motion, you stop being a victim of experience and become an architect of meaning.

Forgiveness as Sovereignty

Forgiveness is not softness.

It is control.

It does not absolve the person who hurt you.

It absolves you from carrying them.

To forgive does not mean to forget.

It means extracting the lesson, releasing the poison, and moving forward with precision.

Holding bitterness is like clutching a blade.

You bleed longer than the one who cut you.

Forgiveness is the moment you stop renting your peace to the past.

The strong man forgives privately, without announcement.

He does it not out of morality, but out of mastery.

He knows anger keeps him reactive.

And reaction makes him predictable.

The man who forgives moves in silence.

Lighter. Sharper. Free.

The Rebuilding

Once pain is directed, reconstruction begins.

The man redefines everything: his standards, his time, his purpose.

He replaces resentment with routine.

He replaces revenge with refinement.

He replaces dependency with self respect.

This is where the next version of him starts to emerge.

Leaner. Calmer. More deliberate.

The kind of man who does not speak about the betrayal anymore because it no longer defines him.

It defined his threshold.

You heal by mastering the lessons the pain taught you.

From Fire to Focus

Pain, once integrated, becomes precision.

It makes a man patient but firm, kind but uncompromising.

He moves more slowly, but with more force behind every step.

He is not easily provoked anymore.

Not because he is numb.

Because he is awake.

He is not afraid of getting hurt again.

Because he knows what to do with it now.

The same energy that once broke him now powers his direction.

He is not chasing closure.

He is creating outcomes.

He is not waiting to be understood.

He is busy becoming undeniable.

Pain is power waiting for purpose.

The Third Law of Betrayal — Transmutation

Pain unused becomes poison.

Resentment wastes energy.

Structure refines it.

Emotion translated into discipline becomes power.

Section 4: The Return to Order

The storm has passed.

The fire burned, the silence purified, and the rebuilding began.

Now comes the return. Most men never make it here.

Not to what was.

To what is.

This is where the man reenters the world after exile.

Not as who he was.

As who he became.

The kind that no longer chases trust.

He creates proof.

The Reforged Man

Where he once sought validation, he now seeks alignment.

Where he once wanted loyalty, he now values integrity.

He no longer measures men by their words or women by their promises.

Only by consistency over time.

That is not bitterness.

That is eyesight. And you only earned it because you paid for it.

Reintegration

Reentry into life feels unfamiliar at first.

He is quieter in crowds, slower to speak, and careful where he invests energy.

He does not crave attention because he has seen what attention costs.

The people who once fit easily into his life now feel out of alignment.

He no longer tolerates chaos disguised as connection.

And yet, he is not bitter.

Just precise.

He redefines relationships not around need, but around respect.

Brotherhoods built on honesty return.

Romantic connections are rebuilt on truth instead of projection.

The New Gravity

Every man who survives deep betrayal gains a new kind of gravity.

It is not heaviness.

It is depth.

People feel it before they understand it.

His stillness changes the air around him.

He is not easily provoked.

Not easily impressed.

He does not compete for approval or react to disrespect.

The man who has mastered pain has nothing left to prove.

His calm now holds weight.

His silence now commands respect.

He does not need to explain boundaries.

They are obvious in how he moves.

He has built a life that requires his presence, not his performance.

Peace as Practice

Peace is no longer a goal.

It is a discipline.

He protects it daily through habits, honesty, and solitude.

He trains not just the body, but the mind.

To stay centered.

Clean.

Deliberate.

The man who once lived in reaction now lives in rhythm.

He starts his day with direction and ends it with reflection.

He stays unmoved by distractions in between.

He no longer avoids pressure.

He welcomes it.

Because pressure reveals whether his peace is real.

True order is not the absence of chaos. It is control under it.

The Fourth Law of Betrayal — Order

Rebuilding from fear recreates collapse.

Rebuilding from clarity creates order.

Boundaries must reflect precision, not bitterness.

Peace must be practiced, not performed.

Section 5: The Oath of Endurance

He has walked through fire, silence, and solitude.

He has rebuilt his strength without witnesses.

Now, standing in the calm after the storm, he knows what few men ever learn.

Endurance is not lasting longer. You quit before this.

It is remaining aligned when everything around you fractures.

Endurance is the law of mastery.

It is what remains when passion fades and motivation dies.

It is showing up when no one claps, staying composed when no one thanks you, holding discipline when no one sees you.

It is the proof of everything he has learned.

The man who endures does not just survive. He becomes impossible to break.

He sustains.

The Oath of Endurance

"I will not let betrayal define me.

Only refine me.

I will hold peace through pressure and patience through pain.

I will rebuild as many times as life requires.

My scars are not reminders of weakness.

They are blueprints of resilience.

When peace wavers, I will return to order.

When order falters, I will return to purpose."

He does not swear it loudly.

Endurance is not declared.

It is demonstrated over decades.

Every repetition of effort, every restraint under anger, every return to calm becomes a verse of this oath.

Reflection

Did this fire harden me, or merely scar me?

Have I grown cleaner, or just more guarded?

When tested again, will I react, or remain?

Because once illusion is removed, a man is left with only two choices:

rebuild with intention,

or drift with awareness.

CHAPTER 12
THE OATH OF PURPOSE

Section 1: The Call to Build

The silence has done its work.

What remains is clarity. Sharp. Clean. Unhurried.

For the first time in a long while, forward motion returns. Not the frantic kind that comes from chasing approval, but the deliberate kind that comes from answering purpose.

He builds the wall to protect his mission from leaking.

He knows what drift feels like now.

It does not look like collapse at first.

It looks like wasted days.

Wasted days become a wasted life.

The Instinct to Build

The masculine spirit is restless in stagnation.

It must construct, direct, or protect.

Without a mission, strength decays into tension.

Without direction, discipline curdles into frustration.

A man without a mission becomes a problem. And you've felt that tension building.

Stillness taught him who he is.

Now building will teach him why.

Purpose Is Built, Not Found

Modern men are taught to find their purpose, as if it waits somewhere out there to be discovered.

But purpose is not a treasure.

It is a construction project.

It takes form through consistent motion, not inspiration.

He stops asking, "What am I meant to do?"

He starts asking, "What am I willing to build and bleed for?"

Purpose is not revealed by clarity.

It is revealed by commitment.

Only by moving, testing, refining, and failing does he uncover what deserves his loyalty.

Direction is not a gift.

It is a decision made daily.

You do not find purpose.

You prove it through repetition.

From Reflection to Construction

Reflection has tempered him, but reflection alone cannot sustain him.

Endless introspection turns peace into paralysis.

The next evolution of calm is construction.

Order projected outward.

He begins small: routine, craft, discipline.

He rebuilds his structure: the morning ritual, the diet, the training, the schedule.

These are not tasks.

They are foundations.

Each act of order declares, "I will not drift again."

Each boundary is a no made permanent.

The man who masters his hours masters his life.

Building becomes proof.

A man who does not build will eventually resent the man who does.

Precision becomes discipline.

Action becomes identity.

The Discipline of Momentum

Momentum is not speed.

It is consistency under control.

He does not need to sprint.

He needs to keep showing up.

The mission grows one measured action at a time.

He learns that boredom is part of greatness.

Repetition is how vision becomes real.

Novelty dies.

The builder remains.

This is where most quit, when results stall and no one is watching.

But he has learned endurance.

He knows this silence too.

He stays steady.

True momentum is invisible until it becomes undeniable.

Building as Redemption

Every strike is repayment.

Every disciplined act pays against the debt of past mistakes.

He does not resent his history anymore.

He builds because of it.

Creation is the only true apology for wasted time.

Each brick laid with intention says, I am not who I was, and I never will be again.

And though the mission begins alone, it never stays that way.

The man who builds draws others ready to follow structure.

Leadership returns not through declaration, but through demonstration.

Purpose creates gravity.

People feel it before they understand it.

The First Law of Mission — Momentum

Waiting for certainty is hesitation disguised as preparation.

What is not built this week begins to decay.

Momentum begins the moment a man stops negotiating with action.

Or he doesn't. And he keeps drifting.

Section 2: Alignment and Direction

A man's peace is only as strong as his alignment.

Without it, even discipline becomes chaos.

Purpose gives energy meaning.

Alignment gives it direction.

The Power of Alignment

Every man who builds must face the same truth: effort without order becomes erosion.

He can work hard every day and still drift off course if his actions are not pointed toward a single aim.

Alignment is integrity applied to motion.

Movement without direction is disguised decay.

It means what he thinks, what he says, and what he does all aim toward the same horizon.

When a man is aligned, his presence feels calm but decisive.

His schedule mirrors his values.

His words do not outpace his behavior.

His energy does not scatter.

It compounds.

The Compass

The man of The Code builds his compass from three coordinates: principle, purpose, practice.

Principle is the spine.

It does not move.

Integrity. Discipline. Truth. Accountability.

Nonnegotiable.

Purpose is the target.

The why behind every action.

The mission must serve something higher than comfort or validation.

Practice is the proof.

Daily actions give form to belief.

What he repeats becomes what he represents.

Principle decides.

Purpose aims.

Practice proves.

When these three align, chaos loses leverage.

Distraction fades.

Decisions become simpler, not easier, because he already knows what he serves.

The Discipline of Precision

Most men chase everything that looks productive.

They confuse movement with progress, action with advancement.

Precision is power: the ability to say no to ninety-nine things so that one thing can thrive.

He learns to evaluate every opportunity through a single filter:

Does this serve the mission or distract from it?

If it does not move him closer to order, it does not deserve his energy.

Every yes now has a cost.

He has learned from betrayal that his peace is too expensive to spend on misalignment.

Focus is freedom with structure attached.

So he cuts excess, cleans habits, and calibrates his day.

He builds guardrails: systems that protect focus when motivation fades.

Vision sets the direction.

Strategy sets the path.

Tactics prove it in the real world.

Saying No With Grace

Alignment demands sacrifice.

The man must say no to comfort, to distraction, and to people.

Not out of superiority.

Out of stewardship.

Every yes to misalignment is a quiet betrayal of purpose.

He does not explain or justify.

He redirects energy where it belongs.

The immature call this selfishness.

The mature call it self-governance.

Boundaries are the wall.

They keep the mission inside and chaos outside.

And when he says no to what drains him, his direction sharpens.

He stops reacting and starts creating.

He no longer wastes time defending his focus.

His results defend it for him.

Integration

Alignment eventually stops being a strategy and becomes identity.

The man no longer balances life.

He integrates it.

His mission, body, relationships, and spirit operate as one system.

He trains because discipline fuels clarity.

He leads because structure sustains peace.

He serves because contribution completes the circuit.

Nothing is compartmentalized.

Every action feeds the same system.

This is the highest form of alignment: when the mission is not something he does, but something he is.

When alignment becomes nature, direction becomes effortless.

The Second Law of Mission — Alignment

Alignment is proven in subtraction.

A mission weakens the moment habits contradict it.

What does not serve the mission must be removed without explanation.

Section 3: The Discipline of Service

When a man first finds order, his instinct is to protect it. You've held it too tightly before.

He guards his schedule, his space, his peace, as he should.

But eventually, peace must be tested in motion.

And the only motion worthy of a disciplined man is service.

From Power to Purpose

The immature man seeks power to dominate.

The mature man uses power to serve.

Power without purpose collapses under its own weight.

It turns inward and corrupts.

But when strength is given direction, it becomes contribution.

The man no longer asks, "What can I gain?"

He asks, "What can I give that strengthens others without weakening myself?"

That question shifts everything.

Service is responsibility with teeth.

He gives from overflow, not from lack.

The disciplined man does not serve because he must.

He serves because he can.

And because unused strength eventually turns against the man carrying it.

Service as Refinement

Service refines ego faster than solitude ever could.

It forces a man to balance authority with humility.

To be effective, not celebrated.

He learns that leadership is not about followers.

It is about outcomes.

The job is not to be admired.

It is to ensure progress continues without applause.

True service removes the need for your name.

The strongest leaders serve in silence because they no longer need validation.

The Weight of Responsibility

Service carries weight.

It demands energy, patience, and emotional endurance.

It asks the man to give his best when no one is watching, and to hold composure when others collapse.

Service is not a gesture.

It is maintenance.

Every system he builds, every team he leads, every person he mentors requires attention.

This is where the mission matures.

Not in glory.

In grind.

Service tests the same endurance betrayal once revealed.

Only now, he chooses the weight willingly.

He carries it because it builds him stronger than comfort ever could.

Service and Boundaries

There is a danger in service: giving beyond capacity.

A man who serves without structure becomes drained, resentful, and unfocused.

That is not nobility. It's weakness disguised as virtue.

That is negligence.

The man of The Code knows that to serve well, he must stay full.

He protects his routines, rest, and solitude, because service without replenishment turns destructive.

He gives deeply, but not endlessly.

Service without a wall becomes self-betrayal.

Balanced service is disciplined capacity.

The ability to give with precision, not exhaustion.

The Currency of Contribution

When service becomes rhythm, fulfillment replaces validation.

The more he contributes, the less he craves attention.

The act itself becomes the reward.

He leads quietly, mentors deliberately, and creates systems that outlast him.

He does not need to be remembered.

He needs his work to endure.

Because in service, immortality is not found in name.

It is found in impact.

Legacy is the echo of consistent service.

This is where leadership and humility meet: when the man understands that his role is not to be celebrated, but to sustain the order he once had to fight for.

The Third Law of Mission — Service

Service without structure becomes self-betrayal.

To serve for recognition is vanity.

To serve with discipline is strength directed outward.

Or he serves himself. And nothing lasts.

Section 4: The Legacy Blueprint

Legacy is not memory. Most men leave none.

It is momentum that survives you.

Service is the act.

Legacy is the architecture.

One helps people now.

The other ensures they keep standing later.

A man of mission does not just give effort.

He builds systems.

He replaces dependency with design and teaches method instead of need.

He builds frameworks that sustain strength when he is no longer there to hold it.

Legacy begins when what you built continues without you.

The mature man aims to make himself unnecessary.

The Blueprint Mindset

The man who builds a legacy thinks like an engineer.

He understands that repetition builds inheritance.

Every standard he lives by becomes a structure others can rely on.

His consistency turns into culture.

His values become unspoken rules in the lives he has touched.

He documents what he has learned.

He mentors deliberately.

He leaves behind tools, lessons, and examples instead of noise.

The blueprint mindset is not romantic.

It is rational devotion.

He treats his daily actions like architecture.

Each one must support weight, not decoration.

Every disciplined act is a brick in someone else's foundation.

Legacy Through Leadership

Leadership, when done right, is duplication.

The point is not to remain the center.

It is to create more leaders who carry the standard forward.

He shares what was once secret.

He gives away the tools he built alone.

He teaches others not just the method, but the mindset, so his philosophy outlives his presence.

This is how masculine order spreads: through mentorship, accountability, and example.

Each man who walks in his stead becomes a continuation of his structure.

Character as Infrastructure

Legacy is not limited to systems or teaching.

It is embedded in conduct.

The man's daily consistency becomes an invisible influence.

How he treats people, how he keeps his word, how he reacts under pressure: all of it becomes a living blueprint for those who watch quietly.

He realizes his example builds faster than his words.

Children model calm before they understand it.

Teams absorb discipline before they can explain it.

Peace radiates outward as culture.

Legacy is not what you leave behind.

It is who you build while you are here.

He knows that when his time ends, the men he shaped will carry the standard forward, not by imitation, but by integration.

The Immortality of Systems

Physical bodies die.

Systems do not.

The man of The Code learns to embed himself in the process.

He builds habits that outlive mood and standards that survive memory.

Whether through writing, mentorship, business, or fatherhood, he converts knowledge into design.

Repeatable. Transferable. Enduring.

That is how a man becomes timeless without needing recognition.

The body disappears.

The blueprint stays.

The wall becomes tradition.

And as years pass, those who follow his path may never know his name.

But they will live better because of his structure.

That is legacy.

Not applause.

Or nothing remains.

The Fourth Law of Mission — Legacy

Legacy is measured by what continues without you.

What collapses in your absence was never built well enough.

What you refuse to systemize dies with you.

Legacy belongs to the man who builds structures that outlive him.

Section 5: The Oath of Purpose

The wall stands.

Not finished.

Holding.

The mission is not a destination. You've treated it like one.

It is a way of being.

He knows the work will never end.

That is the point.

Each act of order is a verdict in motion.

The Devotion of Direction

Purpose is no longer something he pursues.

It is something he protects.

Movement without meaning is noise. And you've lived in it.

Meaning without motion is decay.

So he stays steady.

One disciplined act at a time.

Every task, no matter how small, becomes a devotion to structure.

Every system maintained is gratitude for hard-earned peace.

He works not for recognition, but for rhythm.

The satisfaction of watching order sustain itself.

Peace became possible because purpose became permanent.

The Oath of Purpose

"I will build the wall.

I will guard the mission.

I will serve without excuse.

I will rebuild without drama.

My direction will not negotiate with my mood."

He does not say it to the world.

He says it to the part of himself that once needed proof.

Now, proof is in motion.

The mission continues because he does.

He closes his eyes.

The world is still moving.

So is he.

Not chasing.

Not reacting.

Aligned.

Direction hums like a heartbeat.

The man of purpose does not chase peace.

He enforces it.

Reflection

What did I build today?
What did I maintain with discipline?
Where did I drift?

Correction is due tomorrow.

Without emotion.

Without excuse.

Because a man who builds consistently does not chase authority.

Or he doesn't.

And everything he touched collapses with him.

CHAPTER 13

THE OATH OF KINGSHIP

Section 1: The Weight of Authority

Authority begins the moment a man no longer seeks it. You've chased it before.

It arrives quietly, earned through endurance, discipline, and calm.

True power does not shout.

It settles.

Authority is not claimed.

It is observed.

And when it's missing, that's observed too.

The Weight Beneath the Calm

Authority carries consequences.

Leadership is restraint.

The stronger his influence, the more discipline it demands.

He understands that power amplifies whatever already exists inside him.

If he is selfish, power multiplies selfishness.

If he is grounded, power multiplies peace.

So he treats influence like fire: useful, but never safe.

Because a man trusted with weight can either shelter people or crush them.

Presence Over Position

Leadership born of presence outlasts leadership born of position.

Position requires validation.

Presence commands trust.

The man of presence does not announce authority.

He embodies it.

He does not need to convince anyone he is in control.

His control is obvious.

The room aligns with his tone because his tone does not waver.

He leads by gravity, not by grip.

And when chaos strikes, people turn to him instinctively.

Not because he is the loudest.

Because he is the calmest presence in the room.

That is when he realizes authority is not granted.

It is recognized.

The Quiet Burden

Authority will test humility more than failure ever could.

Failure humbles automatically.

Success asks you to humble yourself.

The man of The Code knows that the moment he starts believing his crown makes him more than those he leads, it begins to slip.

So he stays grounded in practice, anchored in purpose, and surrounded by truth-tellers who are not afraid to correct him.

He does not seek perfection.

He seeks alignment under pressure.

To lead without losing yourself is the rarest strength of all.

The First Law of Authority — The Discipline of Power

Authority must move through composure, not control.

Power is responsibility, never reward.

Influence must grow slower than restraint.

Or it breaks him. And everyone sees it.

Section 2: Command and Composure

Leadership does not reveal character.

Pressure does.

Command begins when others lose composure. You've lost yours before.

A man's authority is measured not by how he controls others, but by how little the chaos around him can control him.

The Quiet Command

Command is not volume.

It is voltage.

The louder the leader, the weaker the structure.

It is the current beneath calm: the energy that steadies others when emotion threatens to scatter them.

The composed man never needs to shout.

Restraint speaks.

He issues direction with clarity, not ego, and because his presence is consistent, people listen.

It is the discipline of full control under tension.

Breathing steady.

Tone neutral.

Posture grounded.

Stillness is not the absence of power.

It is power refined.

Pressure as the Final Teacher

Pressure does not build character.

It reveals calibration.

When chaos hits, the body wants to react.

The heart races. The voice sharpens. Logic thins.

But the trained man does not let biology dictate leadership.

He converts adrenaline into focus, fear into data, urgency into precision.

Where others panic, he prioritizes.

Where others freeze, he moves in small deliberate steps.

He does not need to appear confident.

His preparation already paid for composure.

The Temperature Principle

Every group, team, or family mirrors its leader's temperature.

If he loses control, the room overheats.

If he stays composed, the storm slows.

You can feel it happen in a room.

One man steadies himself, and everyone else gets their breath back.

The man of The Code regulates emotion like a thermostat, not a thermometer.

He does not reflect the chaos.

He sets the climate. Or he feeds it.

His composure gives others permission to breathe again.

This is why he trains daily discipline.

Not for vanity.

For readiness.

He knows that when pressure spikes, he does not rise to the occasion.

He falls to the level of his conditioning.

So he builds calm into muscle memory.

The man who trains composure never needs to find it.

The Art of Response

Composure does not mean staying silent.

It means speaking with precision when others ramble.

He answers conflict with timing, not speed.

He pauses, not to stall, but to ensure truth leads instead of impulse.

He listens fully before deciding.

He waits for the wave to crest before he moves.

Because command is not about controlling others.

It is about controlling momentum.

He does not fight energy.

He redirects it.

That is why even in confrontation, his tone does not rise.

The man who can stay calm under accusation can lead under fire.

The Spiritual Core of Calm

Calm is the stillness earned through alignment with purpose.

The man who knows why he stands does not fear the storm.

The storm only confirms his strength.

Calm command is not apathy.

It is faith in discipline.

And that trust radiates outward.

Others feel it, even when they cannot explain it.

That is the difference between authority and arrogance.

Arrogance demands obedience.

Authority creates order.

Command without calm is tyranny.

Calm without command is weakness.

The composed man unites both.

Direction with peace.

The Second Law of Authority — Command Through Composure

Leadership cannot move through emotion.

It moves through example.

Tone teaches more than words.

Or he reacts. And loses the room.

Section 3: The Burden of Example

Every man who chooses leadership eventually learns this truth: Most men avoid it.

The moment others begin to look to him, his life ceases to belong only to himself.

Every reaction, every choice, every silence becomes part of the message.

He stops living privately.

He starts living as proof.

The Price of Being the Standard

To be the standard is to carry constant awareness.

Where others relax, he must remain composed.

Where others indulge, he must restrain.

Where others speak carelessly, he must measure.

He does not have the luxury of impulsivity anymore.

People do not follow advice.

They follow example. And they notice when yours slips.

The moment his conduct cracks, his credibility collapses with it.

This is the price of consistency: to uphold the very peace he teaches.

The stronger his influence grows, the smaller his excuses become.

The greater the crown, the narrower the path.

The man who chooses to lead understands that accountability is sacred.

He wears discipline like armor because he knows the world tests integrity the moment it sees it.

The Solitude of Integrity

Most men cannot afford that level of integrity.

While others seek comfort, he guards consistency.

While others vent emotions, he absorbs and processes privately.

There are nights when the leader feels unseen, misunderstood, even resented for the standards he upholds.

But he endures.

Not because it is easy.

Because the alternative is chaos.

A man who lowers his standard to be understood ceases to lead.

He finds companionship not in applause, but in alignment.

The mirror of self-respect replaces the need for validation.

And the trust of those who follow is earned quietly, over years of reliability.

The Balance Between Humanity and Example

To lead well, the man must remain human.

He cannot become so rigid that he loses empathy, nor so soft that he loses edge.

He must allow others to see his discipline without seeing arrogance.

To reveal his strength without denying his flaws.

Because the best leaders do not perform perfection.

They model repair.

They show that order is not a state of flawlessness, but a daily act of return.

Example does not mean being untouchable.

It means becoming harder to move.

He shares his lessons without self-pity, his mistakes without shame.

It turns leadership from pedestal into pathway.

When Example Becomes Legacy

Over time, example becomes inheritance.

Those who once followed begin to lead.

They quote his words, but more importantly, they imitate his calm.

He realizes the men he has influenced will never remember every detail he taught.

But they will remember how his presence made them feel.

Safe.

Capable.

Accountable.

When your conduct becomes another man's compass, your work is no longer only yours.

Because now he understands:

the weight he carries helps keep others from falling.

The Third Law of Authority — The Burden of Example

A leader cannot demand standards he refuses to live.

Conduct must speak before instruction.

Visibility removes the luxury of excuses.

Or inconsistency is. And that's what they inherit.

Section 4: Grace in Power

The final test of power is not dominance. You've mistaken it before.

It is restraint.

Power without restraint exposes the man. Completely.

Grace is the discipline that keeps power human.

It is patience in motion, compassion under tension, strength that remembers where it came from.

The Maturity of Strength

The man who has built himself through pain and principle now learns to soften without surrender.

He no longer needs to win every battle.

He no longer measures his worth by control.

Because true control is the ability to release it when peace demands it.

He understands that authority is service, not spectacle.

The moment power becomes personal, it corrupts.

Grace is mastery over impulse.

It is the restraint that allows peace to survive influence.

He builds instead of dominating.

The Restraint of the Crown

Power reveals itself most clearly in the moments it is withheld.

When provoked, the undisciplined man reacts.

The composed man observes, breathes, and decides whether the reaction serves purpose or pride.

Restraint is the refinement of every lesson learned from betrayal, silence, and service.

It is knowing that not every fight deserves your fire, and not every challenge requires your sword.

The man of The Code saves his energy for what builds, not what burns.

He understands destruction is easy.

Construction is discipline.

Restraint is the rarest strength because it cannot be faked.

It is the expression of a man who no longer fights to prove he is strong.

He simply is.

Leading With Grace

Grace changes how he leads.

He stops demanding perfection and starts cultivating potential.

He leads with expectation, but also with patience.

Because real development takes repetition, not reprimand.

He learns that to elevate others, he must lower himself.

Not in status.

In posture.

To listen before speaking.

To understand before instructing.

To forgive before resenting.

This is how he builds loyalty that lasts.

Through steadiness, not severity.

The men who follow him do not fear his power.

They trust it.

His calm no longer intimidates.

It reassures.

That is when he realizes leadership without grace builds obedience, not brotherhood.

The Spiritual Weight of Grace

Grace is the spiritual end of strength.

The point where physical dominance, mental clarity, and emotional discipline converge into peace.

It is the full circle of power: from survival to stewardship, from fire to water.

He has nothing left to chase.

So he becomes an anchor.

When power kneels to purpose, kingship begins.

Grace gives his authority soul.

Without it, he would be another strong man demanding loyalty.

The Fourth Law of Authority — Grace in Power

Correction must exist without cruelty.

Strength must exist without hardness.

Protection must exist without pride.

Or its absence defines you.

Section 5: The Oath of Kingship

The crown rests lightly on the head of a man who finally understands its weight. Most men never do.

He no longer stands above others.

He stands for them.

His power no longer shouts.

It breathes.

The Final Measure of Leadership

The true end of mastery is not glory.

It is responsibility.

Leadership has never been about control. And every time you made it about control, you felt it fail.

It has always been about containment: of chaos, of emotion, of ego.

He carries power like water in cupped hands.

Careful. Humble. Aware a single tremor could spill it.

He understands that the higher he climbs, the more quietly he must move.

The king who rules himself first never loses his kingdom.

This is where legacy ceases to be external.

It becomes spiritual.

A code engraved in conduct, not words.

The Oath of Kingship

He speaks inwardly:

"I will lead without seeking followers.

I will protect without needing praise.

I will correct without cruelty.

I will teach without titles.

I will serve until service becomes my nature."

Reflection

The crown is not mine to possess.

It is mine to uphold.

Power is borrowed.

Peace is earned daily.

My rule will be quiet reliability.

Because kingship is not proven by how much power a man can hold.

It is proven by how little of it he needs to display.

BOOK III

THE BROTHERHOOD

STRENGTH IS PROVEN IN SERVICE, AND LOYALTY IS THE WEIGHT A MAN CHOOSES TO CARRY.

IRON SHARPENS QUIETLY. BROTHERHOOD DEMANDS BOTH HONESTY AND ENDURANCE.

CHAPTER 14

THE OATH OF BROTHERHOOD

Section 1: The Circle of Men

No man becomes great in isolation. You've tried to do it alone.

A man who can hold his house but cannot stand among other men is still incomplete.

Order must extend beyond the self.

Brotherhood is where that order is tested again.

What men fail to build together does not disappear.

It decays and takes everything with it.

Brotherhood is forged under pressure.

Remove truth and it becomes performance.

Remove standard and it collapses.

The Purpose of the Circle

The Circle is not friendship.

It is men holding each other to standard when no one else will.

They do not gather to feel better.

They gather to become harder.

Admission is not automatic.

A man is observed before he is accepted.

His word, his discipline, and his consistency under pressure are all measured.

One failure does not remove him.

Repeated failure without correction does.

The circle does not absorb instability.

It removes it.

The Quality of Men Around You

A man's circle reflects his standards. And your circle has exposed yours.

Surround yourself with mediocrity, and discipline will rot in silence.

Surround yourself with strong men, and weakness has nowhere to hide.

That is why the man of The Code is selective.

He does not confuse kindness with competence.

He chooses men who hold their word, protect their integrity, and move with purpose.

Men who compete for refinement, not dominance.

He does not fear being the least experienced man in the room.

He fears being the most.

Because the room that never challenges you will eventually lower you.

Or he's already decaying and pretending he isn't.

Section 2: The Law of Challenge

Brotherhood is revealed by pressure. You've avoided it before.

It does not threaten the bond.

It proves whether the bond is real.

Without challenge, men decay.

Honesty is the currency.

If you cannot name drift, you are not a brother. You're just someone who stayed quiet.

If you cannot receive correction, you are not one either.

Correction Without Ego

Men break brotherhoods when they correct out of pride instead of purpose.

Correction from ego seeks dominance.

Correction from purpose restores alignment.

The man of The Code understands that tone matters as much as truth.

He does not humiliate.

He hones.

He does not call out to expose.

He calls up to elevate.

The test is simple: does the standard hold?

The strong man's correction builds respect.

The weak man's criticism builds resentment.

And when he receives it, he listens.

Because correction from a brother is belief in visible form.

Challenge and Trust

Trust deepens through confrontation, not avoidance.

Every clash handled with maturity strengthens the bond.

Disagreement without division is the test.

Conflict does not destroy brotherhood.

Cowardice does.

Avoiding truth for peace creates polite decay.

Truth spoken with composure creates durability.

Each time he receives challenge without defensiveness, trust deepens.

Each time he dodges it, the circle learns what his pride costs.

The Friction of Growth

Challenge is friction, and friction produces fire.

That fire can destroy or forge, depending on how it is handled.

When a man of The Code challenges his brother, he expects resistance.

That is part of the process.

But he does not escalate emotion.

He lets truth sit long enough to reveal impurities, not to cause damage.

In this way, Brotherhood becomes a living forge.

A space where every clash polishes conviction.

They prevent the slow corrosion of unchecked weakness.

If no one in your circle challenges you, you are sitting in comfort, not Brotherhood.

If a man refuses correction, he is warned once.

If he resists again, he is removed.

Brotherhood does not negotiate with resistance to truth.

Or it becomes a group of men lying to each other.

Section 3: The Code of Loyalty

Loyalty is the quiet muscle of The Brotherhood. You've called something loyalty that wasn't.

It is proven in presence, consistency, and the discipline of remembrance.

A brother's loyalty is not measured by proximity.

It is measured by reliability.

Not affection.

Alignment.

Loyalty is not agreement.

It is steadiness under correction.

Loyalty without honesty becomes corruption. And you've seen what that turns into.

Honesty without loyalty becomes betrayal.

A man of The Code holds both.

The Three Directions of Loyalty

1. Upward: to The Mission

Loyalty to purpose above personality.

The mission always outranks the man.

If someone in the circle drifts from the mission, correction is not betrayal.

It is service.

2. Outward: to Brothers

Loyalty means being a consistent presence when it counts.

Not constant communication.

Consistent dependability.

When a brother falls, you lift him.

When he succeeds, you do not compete.

You reinforce.

The victory of one strengthens the whole.

3. Inward: to The Code

Loyalty begins with yourself.

You cannot be trusted externally if you betray your internal standard.

Men who compromise their values cannot be loyal to anyone.

The man who lies to himself cannot be trusted by others.

The Line Between Loyalty and Enabling

Loyalty is not blind allegiance.

It does not protect weakness that refuses to improve.

It does not excuse self-destruction.

The man of The Code knows that enabling a brother's decay is betrayal disguised as compassion.

He will stand by his brother in pain, but he will not indulge behavior that dishonors The Code.

Loyalty protects potential, not excuses.

When a brother falls, he helps him rise.

But only if he is willing to stand.

No circle carries men who refuse to walk.

They are released cleanly.

Without resentment.

Without return until behavior changes.

Or you carry men who will eventually pull you down with them.

Section 4: The Fracture and The Reforging

Every brotherhood fractures. Yours already has.

The difference is how men answer the fracture.

No bond lasts without tension.

The question is not if you clash.

It is whether pride controls the repair.

Pride breaks faster than steel.

The Inevitable Fracture

Friction sharpens.

Too much heat, too long unchecked, burns.

A challenge becomes resentment when ego enters the conversation.

And pride, left ungoverned, turns allies into rivals.

Even among disciplined men, fracture happens.

A word said harshly.

A correction received defensively.

A silence misread.

If two men cannot resolve conflict, the circle intervenes.

Not to mediate emotion.

To enforce the standard.

The mission decides.

Not preference.

Not pride.

Resolution is not optional.

Alignment is restored or separation occurs.

The moment you start competing with your brother, you have forgotten the mission.

The Act of Reforging

Reforging begins when one man drops his ego first.

Not in submission.

In leadership.

He speaks first.

He listens longer.

He forgives faster.

He puts mission above emotion.

I have watched men sit across from each other in silence, both right, both wrong, neither willing to move first.

The room does not break from the argument.

It breaks from the pause that never gets crossed.

That is how brotherhood dies: not from the wound, but from the pride that refuses to close it.

Or no one moves. And the bond dies there.

Section 5: The Oath of Brotherhood

The circle stands silent. You know who you'd trust in it.

No speeches.

No performance.

Just the quiet gravity of men who have challenged, corrected, and forgiven one another and are still standing shoulder to shoulder.

And yet, none of them stand above the other.

They form a ring: equal distance, equal burden, equal standard.

There is no leader in this moment.

Only The Standard.

The Oath of Brotherhood

Each man places his right hand on his heart, his left on the shoulder of the man beside him.

The circle closes.

The silent acknowledgment of shared fire.

Then, together, they speak:

"I will challenge with respect and receive correction with strength.

I will defend in absence and correct in presence.

I will honor the mission above myself.

Our bond is not comfort. It is The Standard."

No applause follows.

Just stillness.

The kind that settles when men have said what matters and nothing else.

The Departure

When the circle breaks, each man leaves quietly.

No need for words.

Their conduct will speak.

Each carries the same silent reminder:

Brotherhood is not about being close. It's about who shows up when it costs something.

It is about being counted on.

A circle like this does not end when men walk away.

It travels in conduct.

It shows up in decisions.

It holds when strain returns.

That is the point.

A circle of men can exist without structure.

But it will not last.

CHAPTER 15

THE BROTHERHOOD

Section 1: The Function of Brotherhood

No man builds a kingdom alone. You've tried to.

Brotherhood is part of what keeps it standing.

A brotherhood does not exist because men feel connected.

It exists because standards are enforced between them. And when they aren't, it falls apart quietly.

The Circle is not a gathering.

It is enforced alignment.

Without order, it becomes social.

With order, it becomes generational.

The Mirror Principle

A man cannot see himself completely.

He needs reflection.

The Brotherhood provides that mirror.

Each man shows the others what pride hides: the blind spots, the slack, the small betrayals of discipline.

When one man loses his way, the others close ranks until he finds it again.

Brotherhood is not perfection.

It is correction without delay.

Strength Shared Is Strength Sustained

When men move in alignment, strength compounds.

One man holds the line.

The others do not let it break.

One man's discipline awakens another's drive.

Together, they form an unspoken network of momentum.

A lone wolf survives the night.

A pack survives the winter.

They meet to align, correct, and return each other to standard.

Brotherhood and Truth

Brotherhood fails the moment honesty fades.

The Law of Brotherhood demands speech that is clean, direct, and aimed at elevation, not ego.

Correction is never meant to humiliate.

It is meant to harden character.

The man of The Code speaks plainly not to dominate, but to remind.

Between brothers, honesty is not confrontation.

It is calibration.

Loyalty as Law

Loyalty is the oath of The Brotherhood.

It is not blind allegiance, but principled commitment.

It means: I will correct you privately, defend you publicly, and never abandon you quietly.

Each man knows he is surrounded by others who live the same code.

No gossip.

No betrayal.

No performance.

When one falls, they do not shame him.

They help him rebuild.

When one succeeds, they celebrate without envy.

Conditional Love

A man learns early that much of the world's love is conditional.

Women and children are loved for who they are.

Men are loved for what they provide.

Produce.

Protect.

Perform.

No applause.

No safety net.

Fail, and watch how quickly the room empties.

Often from silence.

Calls get shorter.

Rooms get colder.

Respect turns conditional fast.

Only a tested man recognizes the silence in another.

Only a brother understands what it costs to keep standing unseen.

Men are wired for duty.

Build.

Protect.

Provide.

So we pour ourselves into family, work, and obligation, then look up one day and realize we built everything alone.

But no man carries weight forever.

And when he finally buckles, it is not the world that reaches for him.

It is the men who stood beside him long before the fall.

Brotherhood is not convenience.

It is covenant.

A quiet pact between men who refuse to let one another disappear.

When the world forgets your name, your brothers remember it.

And when your voice weakens, they speak it back into you.

The First Law of Brotherhood — Truth

"I will not seek comfort in agreement, but refinement in truth.

I will study my brothers' strength instead of envying it.

I will carry correction without resentment.

I will be the mirror that sharpens, not the shadow that flatters."

A kingdom of men collapses without truth.

Or it becomes a group of men pretending they're strong.

Section 2: The Circle of Accountability

Every brotherhood is tested not by how much the men agree, but by how well they correct each other when they do not. You've stayed silent when you shouldn't have.

The circle exists to protect alignment.

Not ego.

Not hierarchy.

Not image.

It is where honesty becomes trust and trust becomes tradition.

Brotherhood without accountability is comfort, not growth.

The Sacred Purpose of Accountability

Accountability is not punishment.

It is protection: the shared commitment to keep each man aligned with his highest standard.

The man of The Code knows he cannot see himself clearly.

Emotion blinds.

Routine dulls.

Pride hides.

He will let truth find him before failure does.

Without accountability, discipline suffocates under illusion.

Brotherhood is how a man ensures his standard survives him.

Because a standard no one can challenge is usually just pride wearing armor.

The Structure of the Circle

Every brotherhood that lasts has form.

Clear standards.

Consistent meetings.

Transparent conversation.

They gather regularly, not for ritual, but for rhythm.

Each man reports progress on what he is building: business, family, body, mind.

If one slips, the others respond with precision, not pity.

The circle aligns direction, not effort.

No excuses.

Only data.

If a man consistently fails to report honestly, he is removed.

If he hides, he is corrected.

If he deflects, he is exposed.

Truth is not encouraged.

It is enforced.

Or it disappears.

A circle that protects comfort is not sacred.

It is a club.

No one hides behind mood or circumstance.

Correction as Care

Real accountability requires friction.

The man of The Code delivers correction cleanly, directly, with the goal of healing, not humiliation.

He does not shame.

He sharpens.

He does not expose weaknesses publicly.

He strengthens them privately.

He knows that the measure of brotherhood is not how it celebrates success, but how it handles correction with dignity.

Correction done right is a challenge, not an attack.

The mature man welcomes truth because he sees it as protection.

If a man corrects you, he still believes you can rise.

Pressure means belief.

The Accountability Oath

"I will not lie to myself or my brothers.

I will accept correction before I demand comfort.

I will speak the truth even when it costs approval.

I will never abandon a man still fighting to improve."

When the Circle Breaks

Even strong brotherhoods fracture when honesty fades.

One lie, one excuse ignored, and corrosion begins.

The group becomes social instead of sacred.

The energy shifts from sharpening to sympathy.

He speaks up when standards soften, because silence in the face of decline is betrayal in disguise.

Loyalty without truth breeds decay faster than betrayal ever could.

If a brother continually rejects accountability, the circle releases him.

Not in anger.

For the protection of the standard.

To protect peace, the structure must stay clean.

Better a small circle of honest men than a crowd of cowards.

The Gift of Brotherhood

Accountability transforms isolation into resilience.

Each man inside the circle becomes stronger, more self-aware, more dependable.

He no longer needs validation.

He has verification.

He knows his brothers will not let him drift unchallenged.

This is how men stop fearing the mirror.

That is how brotherhood becomes generational.

In that inheritance, honor survives.

The Second Law of Brotherhood — Accountability

"I will protect truth through structure.

I will correct with respect and receive it without ego.

I will never confuse comfort with connection.

I will value alignment over approval."

Accountability is not surveillance.

It is stewardship.

It is the law that ensures strength does not turn into ego, and loyalty does not turn into blindness.

The circle remains sacred because every man inside it guards its clarity.

Or they drift. And no one says anything.

Section 3: The Balance of Brotherhood

Every brotherhood that endures learns the same law.

Too little pressure creates weakness. You've felt that before.

Too much ego creates fracture.

The Dual Nature of Brotherhood

Brotherhood is not constant harmony.

It is the deliberate balance of tension and trust: the push that makes you stronger and the pull that keeps you steady.

Each man brings a different rhythm: one more assertive, one more reflective, one more patient, one more bold.

When one surges, another steadies.

When one falters, another lifts.

Challenge Without Contempt

Friction is essential, but contempt poisons it.

Challenge given with respect strengthens.

Challenge given with ego divides.

The man of The Code confronts cleanly: direct, unemotional, focused on behavior, not identity.

He says, "You're better than this," not "You're failing again."

He delivers a challenge as a reminder, not humiliation.

He also welcomes the same in return.

If his brothers call him out, he takes it as loyalty.

Because only weak men demand comfort in the place meant for refinement.

Support Without Softness

Balance also means knowing when to build, not break.

Not every battle requires a critique.

Sometimes it requires a hand.

When a brother struggles with loss, fatigue, or doubt, the circle does not lecture him.

It stabilizes him.

One man's steadiness becomes the group's shelter.

They remind him of his worth through presence, not pity.

Real support does not erase struggle.

It endures beside it.

Understanding becomes fuel for respect, never an excuse for weakness.

Respect as the Constant

In every season, challenge or support, respect remains non-negotiable. Or everything turns personal.

Respect governs tone, timing, and intention.

It keeps hierarchy fluid and ego contained.

Men of discipline know it is not deference.

It is discipline applied relationally.

It is the pause before reaction, the calm before correction, the acknowledgment before advice.

Competition among brothers, when tempered by respect, becomes collaboration in disguise.

Humility in Leadership

Within every circle, leadership rotates.

Sometimes the strongest leads.

Sometimes the most centered does.

True brotherhood recognizes leadership as functional, not fixed.

The man of The Code leads when needed and steps back when another is better suited.

He does not cling to control.

He values outcome over ownership.

That humility sustains balance.

No one man becomes the pillar, because all men become parts of the structure.

Ego leads loudly.

Wisdom leads when called.

The Third Law of Brotherhood — Balance

"I will challenge without contempt.

I will support without surrendering the standard.

I will respect each man's rhythm without lowering my own.

I will lead when called and listen when corrected."

Brotherhood at its highest form is not a hierarchy of strength.

It is a harmony of standards.

Each man sharpens the others not by force, but by frequency.

And when that rhythm is kept, The Brotherhood becomes more than a group.

Or it fractures. Slowly. Then all at once.

Balance is the heartbeat of loyalty.

Balance is not maintained by feeling.

It is maintained by correction.

If pressure is too low, it is raised.

If tension becomes personal, it is cut.

The circle adjusts itself.

Not emotionally.

Structurally.

Section 4: The Law of Honor

Brotherhood survives not because men are perfect, but because they are honorable.

Honor is the unspoken law that gives every word, every correction, and every act of loyalty its weight.

The Essence of Honor

Honor is not performance. You know when you've faked it.

It is what you choose to uphold when no one else is looking.

It is the invisible standard that separates men of posture from men of principle.

The man of The Code does not measure honor by approval.

He measures it by alignment.

Does his behavior match his words?

Does his discipline match his promises?

Honor is internal law: The Code that governs conduct when rules cannot reach.

When internal law fails, external consequence follows.

Honor is expected.

If honor is broken repeatedly, the man is removed.

The circle does not carry dishonor.

It isolates it.

The Word as Oath

In every brotherhood, the word of a man is currency.

Once spoken, it must hold weight.

He does not over-promise.

He does not speak casually about loyalty, love, or trust.

When he says "I'll be there," he arrives.

When he says "I'll protect this," he follows through.

A man's word is the architecture of his identity. And when it cracks, everything else follows.

Break it enough times, and the structure collapses.

And when life demands retraction or failure, he owns it openly.

Because honor is not flawless execution.

It is flawless honesty.

Loyalty Refined

Allegiance is not blind obedience.

It is disciplined loyalty.

It means standing beside a brother in public and correcting him in private.

It means defending the bond without defending the mistake.

The man of The Code knows that loyalty without truth becomes corruption.

He will not enable weakness, but he will never abandon effort.

He separates identity from error: protecting the man while confronting the behavior.

Loyalty is not about never leaving.

It is about never lying.

Conduct as Reflection

Honor is not spoken.

It is seen.

It is in how a man treats those who cannot repay him, how he speaks when anger flares, how he handles victory without arrogance.

He carries weight without superiority.

Because strength without humility becomes spectacle.

In The Brotherhood, conduct is contagious.

Each man's discipline raises or lowers the collective tone.

So they guard their behavior not out of fear, but out of respect for the structure they have built together.

Honor Under Pressure

The test of honor is not comfort, but conflict.

When stress rises, when insult strikes, when pride tempts retaliation, that is when real honor begins.

The man of The Code breathes first.

He does not answer insult with outrage.

He does not repay disrespect with disgrace.

He holds line and posture intact.

Honor is the ability to carry respect through provocation.

Because honor is not about being untouchable.

It is about being unshaken.

The Fourth Law of Brotherhood — Honor

"I will guard my word as both weapon and shield.

I will uphold loyalty through truth, not silence.

I will move with respect, even when disrespected.

My conduct will speak louder than my defense."

The Challenger's Creed

"If a man corrects me, he believes I can rise.

If he stops correcting me, I have chosen comfort.

Pressure is proof of belief.

I welcome the blade that keeps me sharp."

REBUILDING A BROTHER

He was one of his soldiers.

By the time he stepped in, the man was hollowed out.

DUI.

No car.

A woman gone—left him for someone she said was "more of a man."

A son he had not seen in eight months.

He sagged under it.

You've seen that version of a man.

The calls started.

Every day.

Sometimes hours.

They didn't talk about the past.

They talked about what was still in his control.

Food.

Training.

Sleep.

Small things.

Things that keep a man from disappearing.

He gave him structure.

A plan.

A place to show up when he didn't want to.

Watch what a man does when it gets hard.

At first, nothing changed.

Then something did.

His shoulders came back.

His voice steadied.

The anger stopped leaking and started moving.

Slow.

Then faster.

He started looking like himself again.

Or maybe for the first time.

He wasn't saved.

He was forced to stand.

That's the line.

Most men don't cross it.

Pity would have kept him there.

Structure made staying broken impossible.

When one man stands, the wall holds.

No one teaches that.

Not rank.

Not training.

You learn it when a man is breaking in front of you and you refuse to let him stay there.

He's back with his son now.

Working.

Training.

Living clean.

We don't talk about that stretch.

We don't need to.

You don't explain results.

He didn't get saved.

He ran out of ways to quit.

Section 5: The Oath of Brotherhood

The circle stands silent.

No noise.

No posturing.

Just presence.

Brotherhood is not a ceremony. You've treated it like one before.

It is a covenant.

An agreement written in respect, enforced by action, and kept alive through honesty.

No signatures.

No speeches.

Only the way they live when no one is watching. That's where most men fail.

The Collective Vow

They stand in that quiet understanding and speak the words that hold their code together:

"I will guard the truth, even when it isolates me.

I will keep my brothers sharp through challenge, not comfort.

I will protect their names in public and their growth in private.

I will remain loyal without becoming blind to truth.

I will never envy another man's rise; I will climb beside him.

I will measure myself not by comparison, but by contribution.

And when I fall, I will rise, not alone, but with my brothers beside me."

When the words fade, the air shifts.

Because one man can hold a line.

But men bound by truth can hold a civilization.

Or it breaks.

BOOK IV

THE KINGDOM

WHEN A MAN BECOMES STILL, HE RULES WITHOUT FORCE.

FAITH CROWNS RESTRAINT; LEGACY IS BORN WHEN THE BUILDER BECOMES THE KEEPER.

CHAPTER 16

THE OATH OF THE KINGDOM

Section 1: Leadership

Discipline shapes the Man.

Order shapes the House.

Authority shapes the Field.

But something governs them all.

Leadership is not a role you receive.

It is a gravity you earn.

It is what makes people look to you when things fall apart because you did not flinch.

Authority is not granted.

It is recognized. Or it isn't, and no title will save you.

And even the man who carries that strength answers to something greater than himself.

That is what keeps power from rotting inside him.

The Weight Beneath the Calm

Authority carries consequences.

Leadership is restraint.

The stronger his influence, the more discipline it demands.

He understands that power amplifies whatever already exists inside him.

If he is selfish, power multiplies selfishness.

If he is grounded, power multiplies peace.

So he treats influence like fire: useful, but never safe.

A careless man with power does not become a leader.

He becomes a larger problem.

Presence Over Position

Leadership born of presence outlasts leadership born of position.

Position requires validation.

Presence commands trust.

The man of presence does not announce authority.

He embodies it.

He does not need to convince anyone that he is in control.

His control is obvious.

The room aligns with his tone because his tone never wavers.

He leads by gravity, not by grip.

And when chaos strikes, people turn to him instinctively.

Not because he is the loudest.

Because he is the calmest presence in the room.

That is when he realizes authority is not granted.

It is recognized.

The Quiet Burden

Authority will test humility more than failure ever could.

Failure humbles automatically.

Success asks you to humble yourself.

The man of The Code knows that the moment he starts believing his crown makes him more than those he leads, it begins to slip.

So he stays grounded in practice, anchored in purpose, and surrounded by truth-tellers who are not afraid to correct him.

He does not seek perfection.

He seeks clean alignment under pressure.

To lead without losing yourself is the rarest strength of all.

The First Law of the Kingdom — Leadership

Leadership is gravity earned through conduct.

Authority is recognized, not granted.

Stewardship turns power into protection.

Section 2: Command

Every kingdom needs a command.

Without it, vision drifts into confusion and strength scatters into noise.

Command is not control.

It is orchestration.

The Difference Between Control and Command

Control is fueled by fear.

Command is fueled by clarity.

Control squeezes tighter when things feel uncertain.

Command opens perspective and redirects energy.

The man of The Code knows that control suffocates initiative, while command channels it.

He does not need to dominate every move.

He creates alignment through presence.

Not micromanagement.

Predictability.

People trust a commander whose tone does not waver.

Clarity Before Volume

In crisis, the weak raise their voices.

The strong clarify their message.

Command is communication under pressure.

Every word must carry intent: nothing wasted, nothing frantic.

He gives direction like a compass: short, steady, measurable.

Clarity beats charisma every time. And without it, men stop trusting you.

When men are afraid, they do not need poetry.

They need direction that holds.

Consistency as Authority

Authority does not come from title or tone.

It comes from consistency.

The longer a man stays aligned with his principles, the heavier his words become.

When he corrects, people listen.

Not because they fear punishment.

Because his judgment has history.

Decisiveness Without Arrogance

Command requires decision.

The man of The Code knows hesitation corrodes confidence.

But he also knows arrogance blinds foresight.

He does not rush to prove certainty.

He acts to restore direction.

If he is wrong, he adjusts publicly, because nothing destroys respect faster than a man who hides mistakes.

Command Through Empowerment

The highest level of command is not direction.

It is delegation.

The great man teaches others to carry pieces of his authority.

He trains competence, then trusts it.

Micromanagement is a symptom of insecurity.

True commanders want their people to grow autonomous.

Empowerment turns followers into extensions of leadership.

So even if he falls, the mission continues.

That is real command: when The Order outlives the officer.

The Second Law of the Kingdom — Command

Command moves through clarity, not control.

Consistency gives words their weight.

The calmest man sets the direction of the room.

Section 3: Legacy

Every man leaves a trail. Most of them lead nowhere.

Some trails fade when he does.

Others become roads, and some still walk centuries later.

Legacy is not what people remember about you.

It is what they continue because of you.

If nothing continues, then nothing was truly built. It was maintained. Then it died.

The true measure of a man is not how he stands in his lifetime, but how long his structure stands after he is gone.

The Two Kinds of Legacy

There are two kinds of legacy: noise and structure.

Noise is recognition.

Achievements that echo until the next louder one replaces them.

Structure is continuity.

Principles embedded so deeply they no longer need your name attached.

The man of The Code builds the second.

Teaching by Transmission

Legacy passes through example, not explanation.

You do not tell men how to lead.

You show them until they start mirroring you.

Your tone becomes their tone.

Your standards become their baseline.

Every moment of consistency deposits a seed.

Some men will not understand what you taught them until years after they needed it.

That is still legacy.

Mentorship as Multiplication

Legacy needs succession.

Without teaching, greatness dies as memory instead of multiplying as movement.

The man of The Code mentors not to be admired, but to prepare a replacement.

The highest form of leadership makes the leader unnecessary.

If everything collapses when you are gone, you did not build foundations.

You built dependence.

Character as Infrastructure

Legacy is not limited to systems or teaching.

It is embedded in conduct.

The man's daily consistency becomes an invisible influence.

How he treats people, how he keeps his word, how he reacts under pressure, all of it becomes a living blueprint for those who watch quietly.

Children model calm before they understand it.

Teams absorb discipline before they learn it.

Legacy is not what you leave behind.

It is who you build while you are here.

The Immortality of Systems

Physical bodies die.

Systems do not.

The man of The Code learns to embed himself in the process.

He builds habits that outlive mood, standards that survive memory.

Whether through writing, mentorship, business, or fatherhood, he converts knowledge into design: repeatable, transferable, enduring.

That is how a man becomes timeless without needing recognition.

The body disappears.

The blueprint stays.

The wall becomes tradition.

The Third Law of the Kingdom — Legacy

Legacy is measured by what continues without you.

What collapses in your absence was never built well enough.

What you refuse to systemize dies with you.

Legacy belongs to the man who builds structures that outlive him.

Section 4: The Corruption of Power

Power does not collapse loudly. You won't notice when it starts.

It erodes quietly.

Not when a man is weak, but when he is no longer being tested.

This is the danger of the crown.

Not losing it.

Forgetting what it was built to carry.

The Subtle Shift

Corruption does not begin with arrogance.

It begins with comfort inside authority.

Decisions come easier.

Resistance fades.

Results arrive without cost.

And slowly, the edge dulls.

He corrects less.

He tolerates more.

He lets small deviations pass because nothing breaks immediately.

Nothing breaks. Until everything does.

That is the problem.

Drift at this level does not announce itself.

It compounds.

When Control Replaces Stewardship

The immature man seeks control because he lacks it.

The undisciplined man loses control because he cannot hold it.

The dangerous man is the one who has control and begins to prefer it.

He stops building leaders and starts directing outcomes.

He stops teaching principles and starts issuing answers.

Everything still works.

But it no longer lives.

The structure no longer stands on principle.

It stands on him.

The Inflation of Identity

Power does not create arrogance.

It removes the resistance that kept arrogance in check.

Without friction, identity expands.

He begins to believe his presence is required.

He begins to believe his judgment is sufficient.

He begins to believe his standard is final.

Correction slows because no one challenges him.

Friction disappears because no one resists him.

And the man who once aligned to law begins to replace it.

That is the quietest failure.

A man becomes the thing his own structure was meant to outgrow.

The Decay of Legacy

Legacy does not fail when a man leaves.

It fails when everything tightens without him.

If no one can stand in his absence, he did not build strength.

He built reliance.

If the system weakens when he steps away, it was never structured.

It was managed.

Control produces dependence.

Dependence produces fragility.

Fragility guarantees collapse.

The Return to Discipline

The man of The Code sees this before it becomes visible.

He does not wait for failure to expose it.

He audits himself with the same precision he used to build.

Where has my standard softened?

Where have I allowed what I once corrected?

Where have I made myself necessary where I should have made others capable?

The Law of Power

Power must never become personal.

Authority must remain anchored in principle.

Structure must outlive the man who built it.

And most men stop correcting themselves long before they fall. That's why the fall feels sudden.

Section 5: The Oath of The Kingdom

The air of the kingdom is quiet.

Not from silence.

From steadiness.

The man stands where his path began, but everything around him has changed. And you know where you compromised.

What once required effort now moves by rhythm.

He looks at The Order he built.

And he realizes this was never about power.

It was about preservation: of law, of legacy, of order sustained.

A steward is measured by what remains calm under his care.

The Steward's Understanding

He finally understands that everything he leads is temporary.

His authority.

His strength.

Even his name.

But what he creates through discipline continues.

The true king leads not to be served, but to serve structure.

He builds laws strong enough to outlive his presence.

He leaves clarity instead of dependence.

He leads so that others never again need to be led blindly.

The Oath of The Kingdom

He places his hand over his chest, the only throne that matters, and speaks inwardly:

"I will lead with calm and serve with strength.

I will hold command through clarity, not control.

I will measure greatness by continuity, not recognition.

I will live so that when I am gone, order remains.

Because if it depends on me alone, it dies with me.

And I will pass my law to those who still rise, so that peace will never depend on my name."

He exhales slowly.

Not an end.

A passing of flame.

The kingdom stands.

And the man becomes its keeper, not its ruler.

THE LAW BEYOND THE MAN

All law begins in order.

The highest law stands above it.

A man's code shapes the world he governs,

yet even he must bow to what no hand can command.

Call it God.

Call it Truth.

It is the force beneath discipline,

the silence beneath will.

The man who lives by The Code does not control this law.

He aligns with it.

The Kingdom is not built on certainty.

It is sustained by faith.

CHAPTER 17

THE LAW OF ETERNITY

Section 1: The Law of Eternity

All things return to stillness.

Kingdoms. Names. Bodies.

Even the man who built them.

Only what aligns with truth remains.

All things return to stillness. You pretend you have more time.

Only what aligns with truth remains.

The man of The Code understands mortality is not defeat.

It is an invitation.

Build what decay cannot touch.

He builds what remains.

Time cannot erase what is built in rhythm with eternity.

Everything else disappears. Including you.

The Nature of the Eternal

The Eternal Law is older than doctrine.

It is order itself.

Discipline.

Integrity.

Service.

Stillness.

These are not inventions.

They are rediscoveries.

All men die.

Only law continues.

He realizes he was never inventing The law.

He was aligning with it.

Each act of alignment brought him closer to the pattern.

Harmony With Order

To live by the Eternal Law is to live in harmony with reality.

No resentment toward what is.

No arrogance toward what is not.

He no longer fights circumstance.

He works through it with precision.

This harmony gives him power greater than resistance: the ability to move through chaos untouched.

He commands not by force, but by constancy.

The man of The Code no longer seeks control.

Transcendence of Identity

At this level, identity itself becomes light enough to release.

He no longer needs titles, validation, or the armor of being seen as strong.

He leads without needing followers.

He creates without craving credit.

He has become what the ancients meant by mastery of self.

He no longer reacts.

He responds.

Peace Beyond Achievement

The man of The Code does not chase more.

He refines what is already his: his rhythm, his reason, his peace.

Where others seek excitement, he seeks alignment.

Peace mastered becomes the highest form of achievement.

Peace is not the absence of struggle.

It is alignment with purpose.

He no longer fears time.

He uses it deliberately.

The Laws of Eternity

The First Law of Eternity: Alignment

What is resisted creates friction.

What is aligned creates peace.

The Second Law of Eternity: Continuation

What does not outlast the man was never built with truth.

The Third Law of Eternity: Release

What is not released becomes a chain.

Section 2: The Legacy of Presence

A man's life will end.

Yours will not be an exception.

His presence does not have to.

Presence is more than proximity.

When a man has lived in alignment long enough, that frequency becomes permanent.

Those who knew him do not just remember his words.

They feel his rhythm.

The way he paused before reacting.

The way he led through calm.

The way his silence made weaker men measure themselves.

That is the inheritance a man should want to leave.

Echoes of Alignment

When a man lives in rhythm with truth, that rhythm imprints itself on others.

A son who rises early without knowing why.

A student who steadies his breath before speaking.

A friend who chooses principle over impulse.

Each one carries an echo.

Fragments of the Eternal Law woven into behavior.

The Architecture of Influence

Physical monuments crumble.

Behavioral architecture endures.

Every system the man of The Code built continues operating even when his voice is gone.

The household still rises early.

The circle still speaks with honesty.

The kingdom still measures success by order, not applause.

Presence sustained by principle does not die. Weak men leave nothing that lasts.

It becomes structure.

The Silent Teacher

The man of The Code teaches most in silence.

His memory does not comfort.

It calibrates.

When those he leads falter, they do not ask, "What would he do?"

They remember how he did everything.

In this way, he continues leading without needing voice or visibility.

Absence becomes guidance when life itself is lived in truth.

The Living Flame

Every generation rekindles what he began.

The students he refined become teachers themselves.

The leaders he forged create their own structures of integrity.

The Brotherhood he built expands across eras, yet remains the same at its essence.

The law continues because it was never his to own.

Only to carry forward.

The Eternal Flame does not belong to any man.

It belongs to The Order itself.

Reflection

If I disappeared tomorrow, what continues because of me?

Are my systems strong enough to stand without my presence?

Have I built dependence or discipline in others?

Or does it vanish the moment you do?

FATHER'S OATH

The room went quiet when she was born.

No gunfire.

No shouting.

No orders.

Just a cry that cut through everything he thought he knew about strength.

They placed her in his arms.

She weighed almost nothing. And suddenly everything did.

For the first time in his life, nothing in him needed to prove anything.

The edge didn't leave.

It turned.

For the first time, his strength wasn't his.

It was hers.

She became his still point.

In her presence, noise lost authority.

In her need, direction became absolute.

He did not soften.

He became precise.

Not indulgence.

Protection.

Not comfort.

Structure that holds.

The world would deny her soon enough.

He wouldn't.

Everything before this had been survival.

This required restraint.

Holding her, something settled.

Discipline stopped being effort.

It became devotion

Every scar had led here.

To build something gentle in a world that isn't.

Strength that does not kneel before innocence is not strength.

It's armor.

And armor does not raise anything.

He didn't lead with force.

He didn't need to.

Presence was enough.

Steady.

Firm.

Unmoved.

Through him, she would learn what order feels like before she ever has to face chaos.

Section 3: The Law of Return

Everything built in truth returns to stillness. Holding what was never yours.

And so it is with the man who has lived fully by The Code.

His motion.

His mastery.

His influence.

All of it returns to the origin from which it came.

Silence.

The Cycle of Completion

The man of The Code once believed progress meant constant forward motion.

He built, refined, commanded, and expanded.

Each stage reached toward purpose.

But in time, he discovers that true completion is not linear.

It is circular.

The leader returns to the student.

The teacher returns to the listener.

The warrior returns to peace.

Surrender Without Loss

Return is not retreat.

It is the release of what no longer needs to be held.

The man of The Code does not cling to his power or his wisdom.

He lets them circulate freely.

He knows that all law is borrowed, all influence is temporary, and all mastery is meant to dissolve back into the whole.

The final discipline is surrender. Or you cling until it's taken from you.

This surrender is not weakness.

It is the understanding that nothing real can be lost, because truth is self-sustaining.

What he built continues because it was never his alone.

He simply carried the pattern for a while.

The Mirror of Stillness

In stillness, he sees himself clearly for the first time.

Not as the builder.

Not as the father.

Not as the brother.

Not as the leader.

But as the awareness beneath them all.

He realizes The Code was never external.

It was reflection itself.

Every law he lived by pointed him back inward.

Toward discipline as devotion.

Toward order as the expression of being awake.

Union With the Source

The man's individual rhythm blends back into the greater order that guided him all along.

He no longer distinguishes between his calm and the calm.

He has become part of the same eternal current that moved through him from the beginning.

He does not need to move to prove he is alive.

He no longer needs to be remembered to remain.

The Silence That Speaks

The man of The Code leaves no speech.

No final command.

His silence teaches louder than speech.

His calm becomes an inheritance.

Those who follow him feel the same stillness guiding them.

A quiet knowing that everything returns to balance in time.

And as his rhythm fades from the world, it does not end.

It expands.

The Code continues as direction felt in every disciplined heart.

The Code ends where it began.

In order.

In calm.

In eternity.

Reflection

What am I still clinging to that was only borrowed?

Where does ego still seek ownership of what was never mine?

Can I release control without losing composure?

If this were my final season, would I stand at peace with it?

Section 4: The Oath of Eternity

Silence settles. And there's nothing left to hide behind.

The world still moves, but he no longer races it.

He has built.

Led.

Lost.

Returned.

Now all that remains is alignment.

The heartbeat between action and eternity.

And in that stillness, he finally understands that The Code was never about perfection.

It was about becoming a vessel through which order could pass.

The man who lives by law becomes part of what endures.

The Recognition

He remembers every vow.

The Law of the Self.

The House.

The Brotherhood.

The Kingdom.

Each one carried him closer to this place.

Discipline became devotion.

Devotion became peace.

Peace became permanence.

The Oath of Eternity

He speaks inwardly:

'I have built with discipline, led with calm, and returned with reverence.

I have guarded peace where others chased noise.

I have treated time as a teacher, not a tyrant.

I have seen that strength without stillness is blindness, and stillness without purpose is decay.

I have learned that every law was written not to control, but to remember.

I am no longer striving to become the man.

I am part of The Order itself."

He bows.

The Circle closes.

The Law holds.

And if it doesn't live in you, it ends with you.

Section 5: The Burden of the Law

The Law has now been revealed.

Not invented.

Not granted.

It existed before you opened this book, and it will remain long after it is closed.

Discipline.

Truth.

Responsibility.

Leadership.

These are not preferences.

They are laws.

A man may ignore them.

He may argue against them.

He may pretend they no longer apply to him.

The law does not debate.

It waits.

Sooner or later every man meets the result of the standards he chose to live by.

It begins the moment a man stops enforcing it in himself.

The Law never weakens.

Only the man carrying it.

Which is why the responsibility is simple.

Carry it in conduct.

Not in speech.

Not in image.

In the way you work.

In the way you lead.

In the way you stand when pressure arrives.

No one else can enforce this for you.

No system will demand it.

No crowd will reward it.

Most men will live without it.

The few who refuse to abandon it change the world around them.

They do not announce the law.

They live it.

The Law was always there.

Now it is yours to carry.

RETURN TO STILLNESS

He had been humiliated by men he once trusted.

He didn't answer with noise.

He stepped back.

The rage came first.

Hot. Immediate.

Then the deeper cut—

not the betrayal,

the silence that allowed it.

He wanted to answer it.

To speak.

To tear something down so the weight would move.

You've been there.

He didn't.

He held.

Somewhere between fury and discipline, it turned.

Revenge keeps the wound open.

Bleeding men don't win.

So he stood still.

And let it burn.

No distraction.

No performance.

No audience.

Just heat, and the decision not to move with it.

Most men fail there.

They act.

They speak.

They make it worse.

He didn't.

He refused to become what the moment demanded.

That's the line.

Few cross it.

The fire didn't break him.

It removed what couldn't hold.

After that, things changed.

He stopped explaining.

Stopped reaching.

The circle tightened.

Not out of bitterness.

Out of precision.

Emotion still came.

It just didn't lead.

Not suppression.

Control.

Very few men stay standing when pressure hits.

So he became one who does.

No announcement.

No correction of others.

Just alignment.

When no one stood beside him, he stayed where he was.

The anger passed.

The structure didn't.

From that night forward, his peace wasn't something he hoped for.

It was something he enforced.

EPILOGUE — THE CODE ETERNAL

The Code does not end.

It is carried.

Not in words.

In conduct.

Nothing remains to be proven.

Only what remains when no one is watching.

FINAL BENEDICTION

Nothing new is added.

Only remembered.

The work continues.

Quietly.

When noise rises, return to stillness.

When pressure builds, hold the line.

THE STILL MAN

When the noise fades, one question remains:

Did he hold the line.

Not perfectly.

Not loudly.

Just where chaos meets order.

He fought.

Built.

Lost.

Returned.

And in time, something in him stopped moving.

Not frozen.

Set.

He speaks less.

Holds more.

Protects what does not announce itself.

Strength is no longer force.

It is steadiness.

He stands in it. Only alignment.

The Code does not live in him.

He lives in it.

THE MIRROR

Read one Book.

Sit with it.

Answer slowly.

Not to impress, but to confront what you already know.

The Code is not learned through reading.

It is proven through recognition.

BOOK I: THE CODE

The Law of Self Mastery

1. What habits, thoughts, or comforts keep you from stillness?

2. When no one is watching, what law do you still obey, and why?

3. Where does your discipline come from: fear, pride, or purpose?

4. How do you react when control is taken from you?

5. If everything external vanished, what would remain to make you a man?

BOOK II: THE HOUSE

The Law of Order

1. What part of your life is built on sand, and what would collapse if you stopped holding it up?

2. What version of you runs your household: the leader, the child, or the ghost?

3. Where does chaos live in your daily structure, and what must die to remove it?

4. How do you measure your leadership when no one thanks you?

5. What are you building that will still stand when you are gone?

BOOK III: THE BROTHERHOOD

The Law of Loyalty

1. Who truly knows you, not the mask, but the man beneath it?

2. Do you hold your brothers accountable, or do you protect their weakness?

3. When was the last time you reached for a brother who was falling?

4. How do you respond when the world forgets you: withdraw or stand taller?

5. What oath have you made to your brothers that you have yet to fulfill?

BOOK IV: THE KINGDOM

The Law of Legacy

1. What will outlive you because of your actions?

2. Does your daughter, son, or family know what you stand for, or only what you do?

3. What would your name mean if it were carved into stone today?

4. How do you honor the divine order beyond your own understand-
    ing?

5. If peace is the proof of strength, does your life show it?

Closing Instruction

Do not rush these questions.

Return to them yearly.

A man does not finish The Code.

He revisits it as he becomes it.

Perfection is not required.

Alignment is.

LETTERS TO MY BROTHERS

To The Man Who's Angry

Anger is unused power.

Turn it into motion.

Forge it into iron.

Speak softly.

Move deliberately.

And the world will quiet around you.

To The Man Who's Numb

You have been hit too many times to feel.

It is not weakness.

It is residue.

Start small.

Eat.

Move.

Sleep.

Pray.

Stillness returns when your word becomes reliable again.

To The Man Who's Lost

Do not chase clarity.

Build consistency.

Clarity follows disciplined men.

One morning, after a thousand ordinary days, you will realize you became who you were searching for.

To The Man Who's Alone

Walking alone does not mean you are broken.

It is how iron is tempered.

But do not mistake isolation for strength.

When you are ready, find your brothers.

The wall does not stand with one stone.

To The Man Who's Ready

The world does not need louder men.

It needs still ones.

Quiet your mind.

Sharpen your discipline.

Do not try to change the world.

Hold the line in yours.

Hold the line.

Or watch everything you built fall without you.